COTTAGES
CABINS

AND UNIQUE RETREATS

COTTAGES
CABINS

AND UNIQUE RETREATS

Editors of **Fine Homebuilding**

The Taunton Press

The Taunton Press, Inc.
63 South Main Street
Newtown, CT 06470-2344
Email: tp@taunton.com

Editor: Peter Chapman, Christina Glennon
Jacket/Cover design: Andrew Welyczko
Interior design: Rita Sowins / Sowins Design
Layout: Barbara Cottingham
Front cover photo: Anice Hoachlander
Back cover photos: Top left: Rob Yagid, top right: Anice Hoachlander, bottom: Susan Teare
Half-title page photo: Susan Teare
Title page facing photo: Rob Yagid
Facing page photo: Aaron Fagan
Contents page photo: Anice Hoachlander
Introduction photo p. 3: Michael Stadler (courtesy of the homeowners), p. 4 (top): Warren Jagger, drawing (bottom left): Christopher Mills, photo (bottom right): Rob Yagid, p. 5 photos: Rob Yagid

The following names/manufacturers appearing in *Cottages, Cabins, and Unique Retreats* are trademarks: American Clay®, Andersen®, Benjamin Moore®, Benjamin Obdyke®, Bosch®, ColorKote®, Cor-A-Vent®, Expand Furniture®, FabCab®, Fein®, Galvalume®, HeadLok®, IKEA®, Kawneer®, Liebherr®, Lucite®, Marvin®, Metro Screenworks®, Miele®, Porcher®, Safest Stripper®, Simpson Strong-Tie®, SketchUp®, Sun-Mar®, TimberCab®, TimberLok®, Vermont Castings®, View Rail®, Wittus®, Wolf®, Zehnder®, Zip System®

ISBN: 978-1-64155-197-7

Library of Congress Control Number: 2023902946

Printed in the United States of America
10 9 8 7 6 5 4 3 2 1

This book is compiled from articles that originally appeared in *Fine Homebuilding* magazine. Unless otherwise noted, construction costs listed were current at the time the articles first appeared.

Homebuilding is inherently dangerous. From accidents with power tools to falls from ladders, scaffolds, and roofs, builders risk serious injury and even death. We try to promote safe work habits throughout this book, but what is safe for one person under certain circumstances may not be safe for you under different circumstances. So don't try anything you learn about here (or elsewhere) unless you're certain that it is safe for you. If something about an operation doesn't feel right, don't do it. Look for another way. Please keep safety foremost in your mind whenever you're working.

ACKNOWLEDGMENTS

SPECIAL THANKS TO THE AUTHORS, EDITORS, ART DIRECTORS, COPY EDITORS, and other staff members of *Fine Homebuilding* who contributed to the development of the articles in this book.

CONTENTS

PART 3: OTHER SMALL STRUCTURES

DISTINCTIVE DESIGNS ABOUND FOR EVERY HOME

Today's cottages and cabins bring unique aesthetics into the mainstream homebuilding landscape

LIVING SPACES CAN CAPTURE THE PERSONALITIES of the families who inhabit them like nothing else. While a dwelling should obviously serve the purpose of providing a comfortable and safe home, form doesn't always have to follow function. Very often, the two marry into a cohesive expression of utility and beauty combined.

While any standard home can be designed or retrofitted to create a comfortable, unique space, there are some types of homes that naturally provide such an environment. Many homeowners turn to the cozy aesthetic of a cottage or the rustic charm of a cabin or look to nontraditional living spaces like renovated barns or schoolhouses when searching for inspiration for their next design project. These spaces, while unique, also boast timeless design elements that transcend trends and capture the imagination of architects, designers, homebuilders, and DIYers alike.

Take the modest cottage, for example. Originating in the Middle Ages, predominantly in England, cottages were first built as residences for farmers and their families. They were small homes, consisting of just a couple of rooms that provided an unassuming and functional living space. Over time, cottages began popping up along the coast of England and began to appeal to vacationers as well as working families.

Today, cottages are a ubiquitous part of the homebuilding landscape, having gained popularity well beyond their English roots. You're just as likely to see a cottage on the shores of Lake Michigan as you are on a windswept British isle. Cottages dot rural landscapes across the continental United States, too, showcasing the design sensibilities particular to each region they inhabit. For example, you might run across a stone cottage near a rural Pennsylvania fruit farm just as easily as you'd find a salt-streaked clapboard cottage on the coast of Oregon.

The thread running through the story of the traditional cottage is the appreciation for a smaller, more utilitarian approach to everyday living. Smartly designed built-in cabinetry, compact hallways that provide more square footage for rooms, and windows positioned to let in natural light at the peak of both dawn and sunset are some hallmarks of cottage design. The discreet origins of the cottage as we now know it set the stage for a new wave of modern small-home design.

This design sensibility is not solely reserved for the traditional cottage, of course, nor is the renaissance of nontraditional living spaces. Take, for example, the cabin. Whether constructed of whole logs or trimmed wood planks, a simple cabin also features a compact living space that focuses on maximizing space and functionality.

This farmhouse-style cabin with its wood exterior, dark windows, and soaring gables feels at home in its forest setting. The architects carefully preserved the old-growth trees on site, so the cabin feels as if it has always been there. But inside, an open floor plan, smart insulation strategies, and high-performance mechanical systems allow for comfortable, modern living.

TOP: This long, low Cape Cod–style cottage reflects the homeowners' dual desires to keep the home small and pared down and to provide water views over the dunes.

ABOVE and RIGHT: This modern urban home and its accompanying laneway cottage were built to take advantage of an infill corner lot in Vancouver, BC. Employing the latest building techniques and zoning regulations, the owners were able to create two inviting and innovative living spaces.

The traditional log cabin goes back as far as the Bronze Age, when primitive cabins started popping up in Scandinavia and other parts of Northern Europe. Constructed of whole logs, the structures were locked in at the building's corners with notches set to stack the logs crosswise. Gaps or holes were filled in with mud or moss, helping to create an airtight seal to ensure dryness and warmth inside.

Today's cabins are certainly not as rudimentary, and not solely constructed of whole logs. It's just as common to see a sophisticated design with high-end materials as it is to see a traditional

The large living-room windows maintain this home's ties to its rich history as a one-room schoolhouse yet still complement its new modern feel.

This compact cabin in Idaho takes full advantage of its beautiful site. The large windows bring the scenery in, while the carefully designed deck extends the living space outdoors without interfering with the view.

"Lincoln Logs" style cabin in the woods, near a vacation spot, or even in a traditional suburban neighborhood. The cabin has come full circle to mainstream as a popular design choice while maintaining its rustic roots. Updated features like open-concept kitchen and living areas, walls of windows to create a plein-air aesthetic, and custom fixtures marry a modern sensibility with the classic cozy aesthetic for which cabins are known.

The popularity of architectural artistry in today's homebuilding market has also opened an avenue for unique and off-book living options that homeowners may not have considered viable in years past. Renovated barns, old schoolhouses, and even silos are now pulling double duty as both primary living spaces and weekend pieds-à-terre.

That's our focus in *Cottages, Cabins, and Unique Retreats*—the new wave of small-space, distinctive homes that marry history and classic design with sustainability and whimsical detail. We're covering the landscape of the whole country to provide a glimpse at regional and climate-specific building materials and considerations. You'll hear from builders who have taken on both remodels and new structures, as well as historical renovations and downsizing efforts. This inspira-

tional tour of gorgeous homes will take you to Martha's Vineyard, the forest, an island, and the Hudson River Valley.

The editors of *Fine Homebuilding* have also added bonus material on supplementary structures that can extend your existing small-space living areas like screened porches, sheds, and pergolas. Whether you are building your retreat space from scratch or adding elements to your current home to make it feel like a getaway, *Cottages, Cabins, and Unique Retreats* is sure to inspire you.

Part 1

COTTAGES

CREATING A COTTAGE FOR TODAY

Daring
departures
from its
traditional
form bring this
Maine home
in sync with
modern life

BY CALEB JOHNSON

GRANITE POINT IS A CHUNK OF LEDGE THAT JUTS out into the North Atlantic just south of Biddeford Pool, a community that was once the site of Maine's first recorded permanent settlement and that is now shared by vacationers, lobstermen, and a mix of hearty year-round residents. The geography is purely midcoast Maine, with rough rocks containing the ocean, and waves that roll in and splash high in the air just yards from the houses ringing the point. It's a beautiful and challenging environment in which to build a house.

I met my client, Rick, through a mutual acquaintance, and we hit it off immediately. He had purchased a plot on the tip of Granite Point and wanted to replace the old Cape there with a new but still outwardly traditional-looking home. An experienced businessman, Rick recognized the natural and regulatory challenges in coastal construction and saw in our firm an ability to address them without sacrificing the art of building in the process.

From the air, the point appears as an oval outcropping tethered to the shore by a sandy strip of land. The site on which we built Rick's house sits at the north side of the point. With Horseshoe Cove wrapping the property to the northwest, the Atlantic only a hundred yards to the east, and the waters of New Barn Cove surrounding the point to the south, the house is utterly influenced by water.

REWRITING TRADITION

Rick wanted to capture the essence of a Maine-coast cottage without being overly tied to the constraints of a traditional design. He wanted the house to be all about the view, and he wanted it to be respectful of the neighborhood. A distinct front entry was also a priority.

After a few design schemes, we settled on a traditional New England cross-gable form. This met our goals by defining a clear axis through the building that allowed those walking in the front door to enter the living room immediately and take in the beautiful ocean views visible through the windows.

In addition to the site's panoramic ocean views, the house's floor plan was driven by Rick's desire for informality. The proximity of rooms is based on his family's living habits rather than prescriptive expectations of how a house should be laid out. The deck, kitchen, and living room are arranged for an easy flow between them. The kitchen backs up to the living room to allow the owners to be together during meal preparation, while the less frequently used dining room separates the first-floor master suite from the more active areas. The stairs, laundry room, half-bath, and master bath

ANCHORED TO THE COAST. Perched on a bluff against the Atlantic Ocean, this new home sits partially on a foundation with spread footings, while the rest is anchored to the granite ledge with steel pins.

BUFFER ZONE. The busy living room and kitchen are joined, with the adjacent dining room creating a buffer between those public areas and the master suite.

and closet were placed on the roadside wall, where views were not important. Additional bedrooms and a study are secluded upstairs.

Around the one-and-a-half-story core of the house, we wrapped a lower section for two reasons. First, it let us expand the home's size while staying within volumetric restrictions imposed by the site's proximity to the water. These restrictions allowed no more than a 30% increase in area and volume based on the house that formerly occupied the site. Second, the lower roof on this section helps to ground the building and make it feel more natural in its environment, something I think makes a lot of sense on a coastal site like this.

ADDRESSING THE OCEAN

With a small lot (approximately 150 ft. wide and 40 ft. deep), setbacks in every direction, and a prohibition against disturbing the natural vegetation, we spent a lot of time working on the siting.

We design houses on sites like this for the ocean side. The floor plan, window placement—everything—is related to the ocean. In this case, the best view required the house to be canted northeast, but going just a bit too far would have resulted in the kitchen windows overlooking the neighboring house. That view in particular was carefully calibrated (see "Wisdom for windows," p. 12) to take in only the view out to sea.

BREAKFAST WITH A VIEW. Casement windows that turn the corner and sit low on the kitchen countertop serve up a panoramic view to anyone sipping coffee at the island.

EAT, LIVE, SLEEP

The rooms of the main floor—kitchen, living room, dining room, and master suite—flow together in a progression that reflects everyday use.

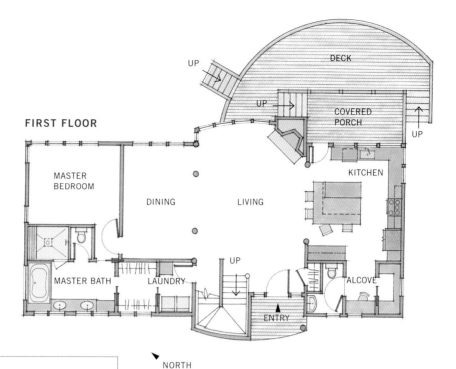

FIRST FLOOR

DECK

UP

UP

COVERED PORCH

UP

KITCHEN

MASTER BEDROOM

DINING

LIVING

UP

MASTER BATH

LAUNDRY

ALCOVE

ENTRY

NORTH

SPECS
Bedrooms: 3
Bathrooms: 2½
Size: 2,500 sq. ft.
Cost: $260 per sq. ft.
Completed: 2013
Location: Biddeford, Maine
Architect: Caleb Johnson Architects & Builders, calebjohnsonstudio.com
Builder: Douston Construction, douston.com
Interior design: Spaces Kennebunkport, spacesnb.com

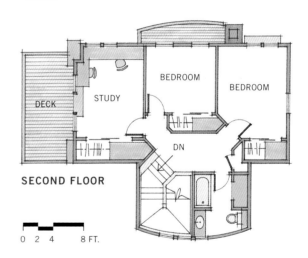

SECOND FLOOR

DECK

STUDY

BEDROOM

BEDROOM

DN

0 2 4   8 FT.

Unable to position a rectangular deck on the ocean side, we drew a curved one on the plans and discovered that by following the arc of the shore, curved decks are a natural fit for waterfront views. What's more, we found that adding a few more gentle curves in the building—in the front wall and the rear wall of the living room—helped the house to sit on the site in a softer way and to feel more comfortable with more space and fewer hard edges. Both curves are gradual enough not to complicate the framing, and the builder, Douston Construc-

tion, had no trouble pulling them off. Since then, I've used similar curves in other projects and have become much less wary of integrating them into my designs.

CRAFTED BY MAN AND NATURE

In addition to the curves, the experience of the house is enriched by allowing some of its structure to remain visible, in particular, the white-oak columns and glulam beams that support the living-room ceiling. Leaving the structure of a

WISDOM FOR WINDOWS

By virtue of its location, this house is all about the views. We took great care in the selection and placement of windows to maximize those views at every opportunity. Here are some of the strategies we used.

MUNTINS ARE NOT A MUST
When designing an oceanfront home in New England, the discussion always arises about whether or not to use traditional-looking windows with divided glass. In this house, we incorporated a lot of open glass without muntins. We found that omitting them allowed for unobstructed views and prevented the building from calling more attention to itself than necessary.

YOU LOOK WHERE YOU SIT
We base window placement on where inhabitants of the house are most likely to be, which means that we calculate our window design from the furniture out. As part of the process, I picture myself in various places in the house and consider: When I look up, what am I looking at? When I sit down, where does my eye hit the window? One result of answering such questions is that we chose casements to avoid having check rails interrupt the view of the ocean.

EXAMINE WHAT'S OUT THERE
In placing windows, we did so with an eye to the composition they would frame. The kitchen windows, for example, were arranged so that the view would take in both the ocean and the neighbor's lovely, bonsai-like pitch pine that lies just outside the house.

BUILD WELL, BUT DON'T SACRIFICE THE VIEW
Having so much glass on the north side of a northern-climate house undoubtedly raises concerns about energy efficiency. Our houses are designed with airtight building envelopes, and they score extremely well on blower-door tests. But when there is a spectacular north-facing view, as there is from this house, I'm not going to tell my clients to restrict glass on that side of the house.

WAKE UP AND SEE. In the master bedroom (photo top), ocean-facing windows are positioned so that the view can be enjoyed even when lying in bed. In the adjoining bathroom (photo above), windows on the wall facing the road are raised for privacy, while windows over the tub offer a full view of the cove.

BANKING ON THE VIEW. Taking advantage of the ocean views to the northeast required a conscious decision to accept the energy penalty the multiple windows would incur.

building exposed allows us to use that structure as decoration rather than relying on applied moldings or other decoration to create visual interest. Beyond the practicality of not having to add to a design, I, like many architects, believe that design is ultimately the act of chasing down some version of truth. Exposing a structure down to its framing keeps me and our designers from fibbing about the building. It forces us to grapple with the details of how things are built rather than assuming we can cover it all up with superficial finishes that rob a building of its innate beauty. There's some practicality present as well, of course. The white-oak columns, which were turned by Steve Hanson of Cape Porpoise, Maine, are not only beautiful in their simplicity and craftsmanship, but they help define spaces, as does the tongue-and-groove white oak that distinguishes the ceilings of the kitchen and dining room.

Outside the house, we exposed the eave to give the low roofs some interesting details, using cypress trim and cedar shingles to take the brunt of the oceanfront weather. I typically use eastern white cedar for exterior trim because it ages so well on the coast. On this project, we upgraded to cypress, which has wonderful rot resistance and fewer knots. It's a great wood to use for high-end trim.

In all my projects, I use materials that will be improved with time and wear, such as stone, wood, and copper. I tell my clients to think of a hike in the woods and the beauty that is found in lichen-covered rocks and old weathered trees. The same can be applied to a building if the expectation of weathering is integral to the building's design. Unlike manufactured materials, which look best the day they are installed and depend on constant maintenance to remain that way, natural materials such as cypress, cedar, stone, and galvanized steel can be left to take on a patina that shows the age of the building in a graceful way.

One of my architectural heroes, Louis Kahn, was famous for having said, "What does this brick want to be?" I cannot say it any better than that. In this house, I wanted to find a comfortable and natural resting place for the materials we build with in a way that would suit their characteristics best. The result is a house that is comfortable on its rocks and welcome to anyone.

A NEW "OLD" COTTAGE

A heritage property in the Adirondacks maximizes indoor-outdoor living space

BY KILEY JACQUES

COMPLETED IN THE SPRING OF 2018, THIS 2,775-sq.-ft. home is located in the town of Lake Luzerne in the Adirondack Park of upstate New York and is the result of a collaboration between homeowners Jeanine and Ron Pastore, architect Brett Balzer of Balzer & Tuck Architecture, and Jim Sasko, principal of Teakwood Builders.

For three generations, Jeanine's family spent summers enjoying the lake "camp" house that formerly occupied the wooded lot. Her grandparents bought the original kit-built house in the 1940s and gradually added a porch and other updates over time. Letting it go wasn't an easy decision, but the old house had reached the point of no return due to structural failures and moisture-related issues. Renovation wasn't an option, so they demolished the old structure to build new.

The goal was a highly functional building that would house and entertain many generations to come. It needed to work on multiple levels, and paying homage to its predecessor was a primary goal. Jeanine and Ron also wanted it to occupy a similar footprint to the original. Other priorities included bigger rooms, higher ceilings, and an upgraded and retrofitted woodstove, which had been the centerpiece of the old house and is an important relic to the homeowners.

The team studied the existing house as they planned the new one. They wanted to recreate what they termed its "quintessential Adirondack lake cottage" charm. Jeanine, an artist, requested a mix of painted walls (for displaying artwork) and natural Douglas-fir walls, as well as fir beams and rafters, which were all treated in a clear stain to lend warmth to the rooms. The window frames were clear-coated rather than painted for the same reason. "Those were cues taken from the original camp," notes Brett. "We wanted to have that warm feel of undressed timber."

They also left the second-story floor-joist system exposed over the kitchen and dining area, which was a nod to the original camp's rafters. Jim describes that part of the program as something of a puzzle. Above the kitchen and dining area are two bedrooms, a closet, and a bathroom.

A SITE TO BEHOLD

To take advantage of the entire site, the home was built next to a hill, which meant thorough waterproofing was needed to manage water runoff at the base of the foundation. In addition to waterproofing the assembly, the design team added a stone drainage swale along the entire length of the house to minimize runoff.

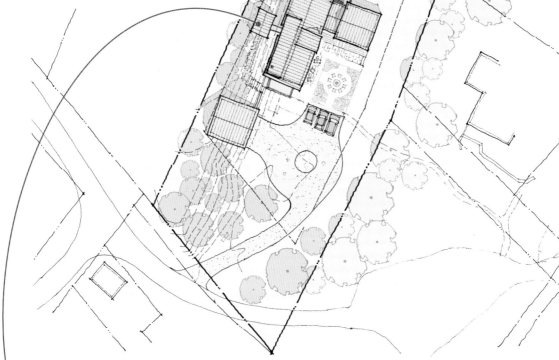

INSPIRED STUDIO

The site plan includes a future art studio, accessed through the back doors and nestled in nature—an inspired space among the trees.

"We thought the bathroom couldn't be above open joists," he says, explaining that the solution was to shift the bathroom fixtures around so they would all be up against the stairwell wall, where they could hide the shower and sink drain lines. All of the plumbing is located in a special section of 2x6 wall. (The rest of the framing is standard 2x4.) For the shower drain, they designed the upper kitchen cabinets to mask the P-trap.

"We saw that the stove would be on the same wall as the trap, so we needed to ensure that the stove wouldn't move," notes Jim. "It's ducted up and out and is hidden behind those same upper cabinets."

Jim also notes their handling of the floor system. Originally, the design called for a thin layer of edge-and-center bead over the floor joists of the exposed ceiling in the kitchen and dining area. Instead, they increased the thickness to ¾ in. and laid a built-up floor on top of that, resulting in an extra-thick floor across the exposed structure. This helped when putting in hardwood flooring nails; there was plenty of stable material to nail through.

Other puzzle pieces included the site itself. The original house was tucked up close to the edge of the woods at the base of a hill, which meant runoff ran straight to the foundation. When rebuilding, Jeanine and Ron were desperate to get away from that hill.

BREEZEWAY WITH A VIEW. The breezeway brings the feeling of outside in with windows that frame wood views and connect the home with its surroundings. An exterior door provides access to the outdoor shower.

"But as we worked through the design," Brett recalls, "we kept pushing the new house back toward the hill. It became a mental hurdle that everyone needed to get over. We knew that we could build next to or into the hill and keep water out. Putting the house back there would allow us to open up the site for a courtyard." The solution included a foundation-wall waterproofing system with a fluid-applied membrane to protect the concrete. A drainage mat was installed over the surface to relieve any hydrostatic pressure while allowing water to move along the wall to a new foundation drain, which then directs the water to a remote dry well. They also put in a stone drainage swale along the entire length of the house. Plus, half-round Gal-

volume gutters capture and redirect all of the roof runoff before it reaches the rear of the house.

Given the ways in which the property is used, the courtyard was key. The community is very close-knit, with multiple generations of families growing up and socializing together. That communal lifestyle figured heavily into the design of the indoor-outdoor connection. The doors to the kitchen and dining area all open to the courtyard to accommodate space for large-group gatherings.

Another important element was the entry; the clients wanted a bit of protection and to introduce the timber that would feature throughout the house. "The big move there was to get the height for the stair once you get inside," explains Brett,

AN INDOOR-OUTDOOR PLAN

The floor plan is designed to connect indoor and outdoor spaces easily, with the kitchen and dining room opening up to the court-yard. The staircase creates a visual separation between the public and private spaces within the home.

SPECS
Bedrooms: 4
Bathrooms: 4
Size: 2,775 sq. ft.
Cost: $456 per sq. ft.
Completed: 2018
Location: Lake Luzerne, N.Y.
Architect: Balzer & Tuck Architecture
Builder: Teakwood Builders

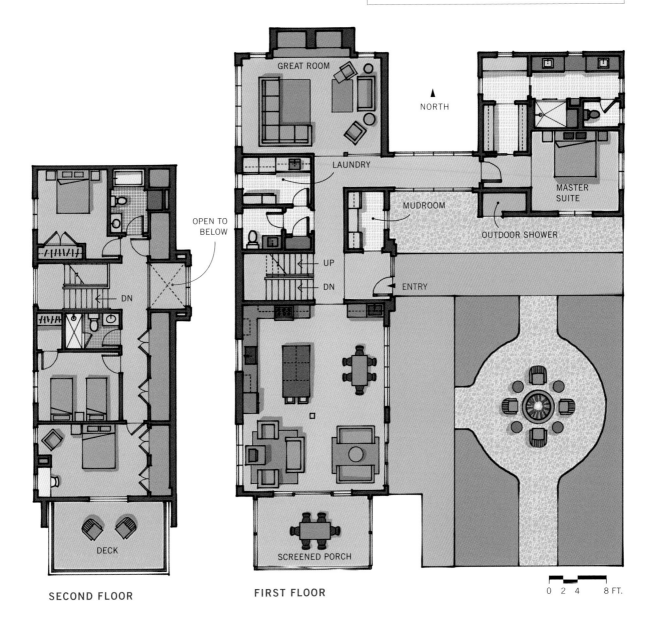

NORTH

GREAT ROOM

LAUNDRY

MUDROOM

MASTER SUITE

OUTDOOR SHOWER

OPEN TO BELOW

UP

DN

ENTRY

DN

DECK

SCREENED PORCH

SECOND FLOOR

FIRST FLOOR

0 2 4   8 FT.

WALL TO WALL. Two different wall treatments lend versatility and warmth to the space. Painted drywall serves as a backdrop for artwork, while Douglas-fir planking with a clear satin finish recalls the original camp's vibe.

adding that the stair hall receives nice warm light that plays along the walls—something the homeowners have come to love. "The irony is that they didn't want a staircase on display," says Brett. "But it became the element that stitched everything together between the public and private spaces."

The stair is poised to be inviting for another reason, too. Off the midlevel landing, a set of doors will eventually open onto a bridge leading to Jeanine's Japanese teahouse–inspired art studio, which will be tucked into the hillside.

Improved functionality makes the new house a well-used, well-loved place. In fact, family members find themselves spending more time there than they had at the previous house. But it's the fact that the old camp's spirit persists that makes it really special. "Visitors often say that it feels like the old camp," Brett muses. "That's the nicest compliment we could get."

ORIGINAL VIEW. A salvaged window from the original 1940s camp house connects the great room to the breezeway. It's a nod to the old home and adds cottage charm to the large house.

A COTTAGE FOR LOW-IMPACT LIVING

This 800-sq.-ft. infill home was designed for its site and its owners' lifestyle

BY NIR PEARLSON

WHEN I FIRST MET MY CLIENTS, JULIE, A VETERAN elementary-school teacher, and Rob, a county commissioner, they had been living in a 600-sq.-ft. remodeled chicken coop on a 2.1-acre property for 28 years. Committed to a low-impact and highly self-sufficient lifestyle, they were on a quest to replace the chicken coop with a simple and sustainable home. Their house would need to be durable, low maintenance, and energy efficient, and it would need to complement their sprawling garden. Most of all, they hoped, their home would inspire them with beauty every day.

Julie and Rob's vision echoed my firm's mission to design sustainable small-scale homes and to promote urban infill. In addition, I immediately fell in love with their garden, an oasis of tranquility and sustenance minutes from downtown Eugene, Ore. My firm's challenge was to design a compact house that would support a modest lifestyle yet foster a sense of abundance.

A VERDANT SITE NEAR AN URBAN CORE

Julie and Rob's lot is a remnant of the farmland that surrounded Eugene in its early days, most of which has since been subdivided into small residential lots. Oriented east-west, the 700-ft.-long lot provides a generous solar exposure that combines with rich floodplain soil to make this property ideal for gardening. During the summer, the vegetable garden provides most of Julie and Rob's food, as well as a surplus that they store for the winter. The lot extends between a major traffic arterial on the west and a bike path along the Willamette River to the east. Immediate access to transportation, city amenities, and the river's ecosystem translates into urban living at its very best.

In addition to its vegetable and ornamental gardens, the property hosted a weathered barn, a storage shed, Julie and Rob's chicken coop, and a bungalow from the 1920s that faces the street and is leased by long-term tenants. With no desire for large interiors, Julie and Rob had chosen to live in the smaller accessory house, and they wanted their new home to occupy the same location among the vegetable beds and fruit trees. Because they spend much of their time tending the land, maintaining visual and physical access to the outdoors was a top priority, so the design of the new house centered on the garden.

SHELTER AMID PLENTY. Decks and porches link the house to the extensive gardens surrounding it, while generous roof overhangs provide shelter from sun and rain.

BACKYARD HOME IN A PRIVATE SETTING

This long, narrow 2.1-acre lot hosts both a main house and the secondary dwelling featured here. Situated between a main thoroughfare and a greenway, the location bridges urban and natural settings.

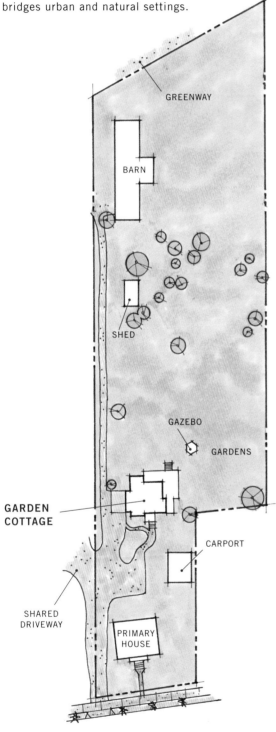

GREENWAY

BARN

SHED

GAZEBO

GARDENS

GARDEN COTTAGE

CARPORT

SHARED DRIVEWAY

PRIMARY HOUSE

Julie and Rob wanted more space than they had in the old coop, but they were content to limit the area and height of their new home to comply with local regulations for secondary dwelling units. To accommodate future growth through greater housing density, Eugene's zoning code allows construction of accessory dwellings alongside existing homes on single-home residential properties. Although the zoning code limits the interior of an accessory dwelling to 800 sq. ft. of living space, it allows this living space to be augmented with covered outdoor areas and storage or utility rooms with exterior access.

We took advantage of this allowance to add a mechanical room and multiple covered porches, and because areas with low headroom are not legally considered habitable rooms, we included a bonus space. This area, accessed by a ladder, includes a concealed mechanical-equipment attic and an open, daylit meditation loft.

DESIGNED FOR THE PACIFIC NORTHWEST

The Pacific Northwest is known for its long, rainy winters, prompting a "shed the water and bring in the light" strategy. Summers can be hot, however, so solar protection is necessary. Generous overhangs on the house's low-sloped shed roofs address all these issues. The south-sloping roof extends the full width of the house and shelters the great-room windows from winter storms and summer heat. It also points two solar arrays toward the sun and allows for north-facing clerestories to illuminate the guest room and loft. The north-facing roof opens the main bedroom to garden views and to mini-clerestories. A small roof on the west shelters the entry. To the south, a roof over the patio springs up and away from the house to frame expansive views and to allow low-angle winter sun to penetrate the indoors. The windows, clerestories, skylights, and three exterior glazed doors provide an ongoing connection with the outdoors and bring in ample daylight.

POWER AND LIGHT. In addition to shelter, the roofs provide a platform for solar panels and a venue for clerestories.

Julie and Rob wanted their home to represent the Pacific Northwest aesthetically as well. Combining modern forms with traditional craftsmanship, this hybrid timber-frame house includes exposed, load-bearing heavy-timber construction as well as standard joists and studs. Posts, beams, rafters, and roof decking were milled from regional Douglas-fir or hemlock timber. The woodwork is clear-coated, which highlights the mineral-tinted Imperial Plaster wall finish (usg.com).

SIGHTLINES AND VIEWS MAKE A SMALL HOUSE FEEL SPACIOUS

Julie and Rob wanted their home to be at what they called a "human scale." Julie defines that as "not so big as to feel dwarfed and diminished, but not so small as to feel confined and limited." With Julie and Rob's human scale in mind, we designed the roof—with its rafters exposed—to define the scale, orientation, and character of each interior space. With no option for vast rooms, we mixed

DURABLE DETAILS

Long-lasting exterior finishes are a big part of sustainable building, and the Pacific Northwest's damp climate can be unforgiving to poorly detailed exteriors. Low-maintenance finishes include copper-penny metal roofing, fascia cladding, gutters, and downspouts. The steel columns are painted to complement the roof. Most of the building is clad with fiber-cement lap siding. This durable, low-maintenance material is simple to install, and it provides a familiar, homey look. Wall areas that are protected by eaves or by patio roofs feature stained plywood. Similarly, the Douglas-fir exterior doors are protected by overhanging roofs. The windows are wood with aluminum cladding.

and overlapped the entry, living, dining, kitchen, and circulation spaces into a great room. Long vistas through spaces, windows, and doors foster a sense of expansion, while coves such as a window seat off the great room allow for repose.

To prevent monotony, spaces are delineated by changes in flooring or with cabinets or built-ins. For example, the slate flooring transitions from the entry into a simple hearth, where a woodstove visually anchors the great room.

THIRD-PARTY CERTIFICATION CONFIRMS THE HOME'S QUALITY CONSTRUCTION

Julie and Rob's commitment to sustainable living allowed us to select strategies to reduce their carbon footprint significantly. This earned their home an Earth Advantage Platinum Certification, the highest level offered by Earth Advantage New Homes, an Oregon-based third-party certification program. Earth Advantage weighs energy efficiency, indoor-air quality, resource efficiency, environmental responsibility, and water conservation.

The roof and walls were sheathed with a continuous layer of rigid foam, 1 in. on the walls and 2 in. on the roof. This foam prevents thermal bridging

DAYLIGHT, NOT CABINETS. Windows bring light and space to the work areas. Storage cabinets cluster on interior walls.

MAKING SMALL SEEM BIG

As an accessory dwelling, this house was limited by ordinance to having an interior no larger than 800 sq. ft. Long sightlines and shared spaces make the public areas seem bigger, while the main bedroom's location off a short hall emphasizes privacy. Decks and porches, which are not subject to the same size restrictions, were used to expand the house both visually and physically. Carefully placed doors and windows provide access to these decks and porches, as well as to the extensive gardens.

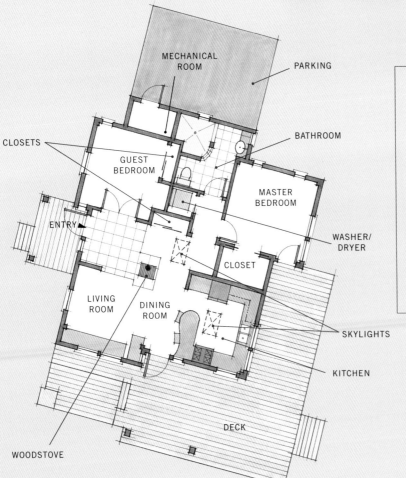

MECHANICAL ROOM

PARKING

BATHROOM

CLOSETS

GUEST BEDROOM

MASTER BEDROOM

ENTRY

WASHER/ DRYER

CLOSET

LIVING ROOM

DINING ROOM

SKYLIGHTS

KITCHEN

DECK

WOODSTOVE

SPECS

Bedrooms: 2
Bathrooms: 1
Size: 800 sq. ft.
Cost: $270 per sq. ft.
Completed: 2012
Location: Eugene, Ore.
Architect: Nir Pearlson Architect;
　　　green-building.com
Builder: Six Degrees Construction;
　　　sixdegreesconstruction.com

NORTH

0 2 4　8 FT.

DELINEATED BY FUNCTION. A peninsula with barstool seating defines the kitchen, while a stove hearth and window seat invite relaxation in the great room. A small altar marks the entrance to the main bedroom.

and insulates well beyond code levels. Daylight from the windows minimizes the need for electric lighting, and a minisplit heat pump couples with a heat-recovery ventilator to heat and ventilate the home efficiently. A woodstove provides backup heat and ambience.

A grid-tied solar photovoltaic array offsets summertime electricity use; domestic hot water is provided by a solar hot-water collector. In the future, a gray-water diversion system and rainwater catchment cisterns will supply irrigation water to the gardens.

Julie and Rob are satisfied with their new home. Julie says, "Our home is the intimate interplay of inside cozy places of sanctuary and outside gardens splashing light and life through windows. The eye and heart dance from one angle of beauty to another as the intersections create a peaceful harmony."

HOME AND BARN: A NATURAL BUILD

Natural materials and ecologically sound building practices define this timber-frame home

BY KILEY JACQUES

LIKE ALL PROJECTS BY VERMONT-BASED NEW Frameworks Natural Design/Build, this two-story, 1,600-sq.-ft. timber-frame home features locally sourced nontoxic products such as blown-in cellulose insulation and lime-casein interior paint. The worker-owned company is committed to the use of natural materials and ecologically sound building practices that incorporate passive solar design strategies. Here, that included glass panels integrated into the porch overhang. They were constructed to take advantage of the low angle of the winter sun, allowing it to penetrate the building and heat the tile floors.

Much of the home's character comes from the many reclaimed and salvaged pieces the homeowners have collected. Among them is an antique soaking tub; it was key to their vision, so the plumber had to determine how best to deliver water to the massive cast-iron receptacle. The tub ended up dictating the sizing of the hot-water system—a pellet boiler with solar hot water supplement—which subsequently drove the decision to add radiant heating. That heating system would not have been a prudent choice otherwise, given the high-performance home's minimal heating loads. The bathroom includes another allowance—the one window on the building's north side.

Designer/builder: New Frameworks Natural Design/Build,
newframeworks.com

Location: Middlesex, Vt.

Photos: SB Studio, courtesy of New Frameworks Natural
Design/Build

SENSITIVE SCALE, MODEST MATERIALS

This Cape Cod home maintains a pared-down simplicity with a low-pitch roof and visually separate forms

BY KILEY JACQUES

ACCORDING TO ARCHITECT PETER TWOMBLY, this project was influenced by a house designed by writer and naturalist Henry Beston, author of *The Outermost House,* which chronicles a season spent living on the dunes of Cape Cod. The new build took cues from the house that Beston designed, specifically its modest scale and pared-down simplicity. In contrast to the regional trend of razing old cottages in favor of elaborate mansions, this structure is actually smaller than the house it replaced.

Twombly says it was a challenge to achieve flood-zone elevations and provide water views over the dune while maintaining the low roof profile that the clients desired. The solution was to divide the house into small-scale, visually separate forms tied together with shared features such as shingles, shutters, boardwalks, and porches. The roof pitch was lowered as far as possible without sacrificing a traditional look, and a stone wall on the entry side reinforces the low profile and anchors the house to the site. To help obscure the flood-resistant pier foundation, Twombly used lattice panels around the base of the building.

"By making subtle adjustments to the grade, emphasizing horizontal massing, and keeping the roof pitch low, the scale of the house meets both code flood requirements and the owners' criteria."

—Peter Twombly, architect

Designer: Estes Twombly Architects, estestwombly.com
Builder: Fellman Brothers Builders
Location: Chatham, Mass.
Photos: Warren Jagger

AN ISLAND RETREAT BUILT TO LAST

A remodel of
a home on
Block Island,
R.I., offers
a classic
look with a
modern twist

BY JANICE ROHLF

FOR THEIR LONG-SOUGHT BLOCK ISLAND, R.I.,
retreat, the clients asked for a modest house that would be inexpensive to
build and easy to maintain, and, given the rugged climate, wouldn't cost
a fortune to keep up or heat. They admired the simplicity and directness
of older farmhouses in the area but wanted their house to be modern and
open. The result is an efficient 20-ft. by 42-ft. two-story block with two
first-floor cutouts: 1,600 sq. ft. total with three bedrooms. An indented
glass wall to the south and west captures the sun and opens onto a large
south-facing deck for outdoor living. With the exception of the bedroom
suite on the opposite side of the house, where views were a must, glazing
was limited to punched openings to keep the house thermally efficient.
Large, top-quality Andersen double-hung windows were worth a budget-
ary splurge for their insulating value. The vinyl trim, shingles, and cedar
on the pergola never need painting, and the metal roof will last for 20 to
30 years. Inside, most surfaces are easy-to-maintain plaster with a simple,
painted trim.

"The general trend is to build bigger and
bigger houses that are not in keeping with
the nature of the place. These clients knew
what it was all about and wanted to keep it
simple; keep it Block Island."

—Jim Estes, architect

Architects: Estes Twombly + Titrington
Architects, ettarchitects.com
Builder: Bannon Custom Builders,
bannonbuilds.com
Location: Block Island, R.I.
Photos: Warren Jagger

LOW MAINTENANCE FOR THE LONG TERM

A low-cost home that requires minimal upkeep offers comfortable living for the long haul

BY JON NYSTROM

ALL OF US HOPE TO RETIRE SOMEDAY. TO DO SO IN the home of our dreams, one that enables as long a stay as possible, is a goal seldom realized. After living for 21 years in New England, my wife and I finally decided to return to her native Texas Hill Country with the hope of building a retirement home that I would design.

Nancy and I found a small plot of land close to downtown Boerne, just north of San Antonio, where we could walk to shops and restaurants; be near our friends, community services, and health-care providers; and enjoy the area's natural beauty. The house we built there is next to Frederick Creek, and when sitting beside it on a swing in the shade, you would never guess that Main Street is only a few blocks away.

Designing our house was demanding, mostly because we knew it would be our home for the rest of our lives. A retirement home is a unique project in that it involves careful consideration of long-term accessibility, maintenance, energy efficiency, affordability on a fixed income, and of course, comfort. In addition to these practical concerns, we also wanted a beautiful home, one that would fit in with its surroundings here, deep in the heart of Texas.

BLENDING INTO AN EVOLVING NEIGHBORHOOD

We built our home in a transitional neighborhood, an area slowly morphing from a barrio of homesteads occupied by extended families into an eclectic mixture of new homes built close together on narrow lots. To build a house in the middle of a manicured lawn with grand details would definitely stand out in The Flats, as our neighborhood is known. However, simple homes with limestone-gravel driveways, corrugated-metal roofs, and stucco walls are common. In an attempt to make it blend in, we built our home with known elements, even if we didn't use them in quite the same way as our neighbors.

We carefully considered the siting of the house as well, and the arrangement of the main house and the garage was made possible by our unique lot. Our site is bordered on one side by a city-owned 50-ft.-wide easement. Not only does the easement protect us from future development on the southwestern property line, but we're also allowed to use half of it for our driveway, which allowed us to turn our two-car, detached garage 45° to the street. We did this for two reasons. The roof is oriented due south at a 30° slope, which is ideal for photovoltaic panels. Currently, only solar hot-water panels occupy the garage roof. We are waiting for more tax incentives before filling the remaining roof with PV panels. The location

COMFORTABLE LIVING FOR THE LONG HAUL.
Designed with an emphasis on long-term livability
and built with regionally appropriate, durable, and
low-maintenance materials, this home is remarkably
fit for aging in place in style and comfort.

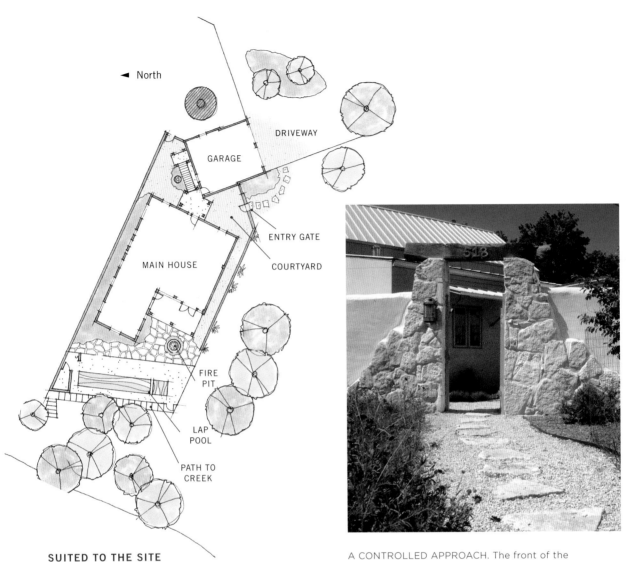

North ◄

DRIVEWAY

GARAGE

ENTRY GATE

COURTYARD

MAIN HOUSE

FIRE
PIT

LAP
POOL

PATH TO
CREEK

SUITED TO THE SITE

The courtyard is more deliberately defined by the placement of the garage in front of the main house and the 6-ft.-tall masonry walls along the property lines.

A CONTROLLED APPROACH. The front of the house is partially hidden by the garage and is accessed by a stone path leading through an iron gate beneath an old mesquite timber and into an intimate courtyard.

of the garage also allows it to serve as a buffer between the house and the street. Stucco privacy walls along the side property lines terminate in iron gates on both sides of the garage. This layout creates an intimate front courtyard between the house and the garage that is private, quiet, and shaded, with the prevailing breeze floating through. With a small fountain that gurgles close by the front door, the courtyard offers a secure, serene feeling as you enter the house.

WIDE-OPEN LIVING

I organized the floor plan so that visitors are welcomed immediately into the house's core: a timber-frame dining and living area with soaring 22-ft.-tall ceilings. The massive Douglas-fir beams evoke a remarkable sense of structure and craftsmanship, but they also temper the scale of the room to make it feel expansive yet comfortable.

The floor plan grows from this main living area and is as space efficient as I could make it. There

THE HEART OF THE HOME. The combined living and dining area is the epicenter of the floor plan and is set before a glazed wall to establish a strong connection to the outdoors and creek basin.

are no hallways occupying valuable square footage or limiting accessibility, and there aren't any spaces we don't use daily. The plan has been distilled to our absolute needs: a master suite, an office that can serve as additional guest space, a bathroom, and a kitchen connected to our living and dining area. The house is just under 2,000 sq. ft., small by some standards, but it feels much larger due to this layout, the volume of each room, the amount of natural light, and the views introduced through carefully placed windows and doors.

The floor plan is also organized to create a focus on the outdoors—a big priority for Nancy and me. Having forgone the Hill Country trend of carving a building site out of a hilltop to capture panoramic landscape views, I designed a glass wall using Kawneer commercial window units to invite the outdoors into our daily lives and to allow the interior living space to extend onto the patio. Beyond the covered sitting and grill area, I placed a lap pool and spa that cling to the edge of the 18-ft.-high slope to the floodplain of Frederick Creek. We will always experience the presence of water, even when the creek runs dry during periods of drought.

SPACE EFFICIENT

NORTH

KITCHEN

DINING

PATIO

ENTRY ▶

LIVING

LAUNDRY

MASTER
BEDROOM

OFFICE

MASTER
BATH

0 2 4   8 ft.

SPECS
Bedrooms: 2, including apartment
Bathrooms: 3, including apartment
Size: house, 1,970 sq. ft.
         apartment, 450 sq. ft.
Cost: $150 sq. ft.
Completed: 2011
Location: Boerne, Texas
Architect/builder: Jon Nystrom; jonnystromarchitect.com

GARAGE APARTMENT CREATES AN ADAPTIVE HOME

Perhaps more than any other type of residence, a retirement home needs to be flexible. With this in mind, I designed the house to be as functional as possible and to adapt to our life as we age. The 450-sq.-ft. fully equipped apartment I placed above the garage is an important part of our efforts to live in this house for as long as we can.

We finished the garage apartment first, then lived in it for four months while we completed construction on the main house, which allowed us to move out of our rented condominium earlier than we would have otherwise. In addition to this early economic perk, the garage apartment serves as a guest space for family and friends. We also rent it out frequently, earning roughly twice the amount of our annual property-tax bill by doing so. As we age, we envision the apartment serving as living quarters for an in-home caregiver while we continue to enjoy privacy and a sense of independence in the main house.

EFFICIENCY ENABLES STABILITY

Energy is getting expensive in South Texas, and we are running out of water—problems that are not at all unique to this part of the country. To maintain a sense of security and economic stability for our future, I designed the house to respond to the diminishing resources in our region.

OPEN ACCESS. The kitchen offers plenty of
circulation space, full four-finger-grip door and
drawer pulls on maple cabinets, and an island
with deep countertop overhangs that can accommodate wheelchair users.

FLEX SPACE FOR LONG-TERM LIVING

Homeowners committed to living in their house for the long haul need to prepare for unexpected challenges and potential services. The linchpin of this home's flexible design is the 450-sq.-ft. apartment over the garage. Designed to be comfortable for short or long stays, the apartment has a full kitchen and bathroom, should Jon and Nancy ever need permanent live-in help. The main living space, which serves as a den, a bedroom, and a dining area, is set beneath a ceiling clad with corrugated metal salvaged from the roof of the house that once occupied the site.

Overlooking the front courtyard, the apartment is isolated but not completely disconnected from the main house. Creating spaces that anticipate the trials of age—without stark reminders of the limitations ahead—is what comfortable, flexible design is all about.

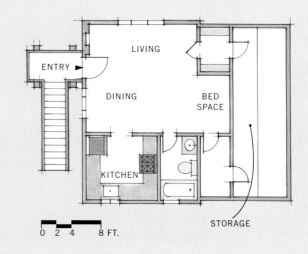

Not only can our roof efficiently accommodate the installation of photovoltaic panels, but we also harvest valuable rainwater from the roof. It doesn't rain often here, but when it does, it's typically a violent gully washer. We collect 1,000 gal. of water with every inch of rain and store it in an 8,400-gal. corrugated-steel tank. Reminiscent of some of the silos in this region, the tank is in the front yard beside the garage. The stored water irrigates the small amount of landscaping that we have on the property and helps to offset the water we consume for our pool.

Our biggest move toward creating an economical and efficient home was to build it with structural insulated panels (SIPs). The SIPs represented a 12% increase in construction cost over conventional framing, but now we have R-19 walls and an R-40 roof. With a tight, well-insulated envelope that minimizes thermal bridging, 1-in. argon-filled low-e windows, and permanent metal sunshades over south- and west-facing windows to reduce excessive solar heat gain, our HVAC system is roughly half the size of what it would have been otherwise. The design of this assembly, much like all the other elements in the house, is intended to yield low utility bills and minimal upkeep costs, which is paramount for our future comfort and our financial ability to stay put for as long as we can.

Nancy and I can't predict what lies on the horizon. Because we put a lot of ourselves into this home, however, we're confident that it's going to give back just as much and take care of us when we need it the most.

DESIGN DETAILS THAT AGE WELL

You can't live in a home for very long if you can't maintain it, so this house was designed to be as maintenance free as possible to limit future expenses and also to accommodate aging occupants.

On the inside, concrete floors throughout the house are virtually indestructible and were chemically sealed as opposed to having a sealer applied. The more they're used, the more polished they will appear. The walls are not painted but instead have been finished with American Clay plaster impregnated with Nantucket Sand pigment in Enjarre finish. The timber-frame structure is made of pickled Douglas fir. The framework, combined with a minimal amount of similarly stained wood trim, enables the home to age gracefully, without the need for laborious repainting. All bathroom and kitchen countertops are poured quartz, requiring no special care.

A similar approach was taken on the exterior. Stucco and metal siding and roofing create a simple, durable exterior shell. There is no lawn, and planting beds that contain native wildflowers and plants that thrive in the hot, dry climate of the South are watered by an irrigation system supplied by water catchment in an added effort to make this home as easy to live in as possible.

100-YEAR-OLD RESTORATION

Lessons in small-home design for downsizing and living well with less

BY ROB YAGID

THE BROMICA SCHOOL HOUSE SITS AT THE CORNER of intersecting dirt roads in Kent, a small town along the Housatonic River in northwestern Connecticut. Constructed in 1920, it was among 14 one-room schoolhouses in service to the region. By 1950, the school, along with only a handful of others left in the area's more remote hills, had closed its doors for good. It since served as a single-family home, but fell into severe disrepair by the late 1990s. By the time a local carpenter and his wife—my parents—purchased the property in 2019, there had been multiple attempts to restore it. The latest, initiated by a local architect who had the building gutted, left them with a blank slate to create a comfortable, functional, and fun home where they could enjoy retirement.

The rebuilding of this home was an exercise in imaginative small-home design, where core living spaces are creatively arranged to make the most of the home's footprint on the nonconforming lot. The upgrades in both performance and aesthetics were based on comfort and a real-world budget, with the intention of giving the home a more modern look and feel without erasing all semblance of its rich history—a practical approach that can be replicated in any project, whether new or extensively remodeled.

A few years ago, my parents found themselves living in a home they loved but that no longer fit their lifestyle. At 3,400 sq. ft., the traditional colonial that my father built many years prior had become much too large for their needs and for how they wanted to spend their time. When most people consider downsizing, they don't quite envision living in a home that's a quarter of the size of their former residence. But the schoolhouse was too charming to pass up. And while small-home living has its challenges, they were more than willing to take them on. A truly small home demands letting go of a lot of material items, keeping what matters most, and adjusting your living patterns. When designed well, however, a small home affords a certain level of comfort that can't as easily be found in larger houses.

Because the house is on a nonconforming lot, no additions would be approved by zoning. There would be no easy outs in developing the floor plan. Fortunately, the existing structure had a few key elements that were retained and enhanced to make it all work. The first was the vaulted ceiling. The second was a small existing loft at the back of the structure, and the third was a trio of tall beautiful windows that undoubtedly once drew the attention of daydreaming students who could gaze up at the tops of the nearby maple trees. It only made sense to anchor the main living area adjacent to these windows—updated with double-hung Marvin Integrity units in the same proportion as the originals—in order to take full advan-

DEFINED SPACES

The floor plan organizes public, private, and flexible spaces amidst the open plan to bring order and functionaily to the design. A large patio steps away from the kitchen and provides an open area for entertaining friends and family.

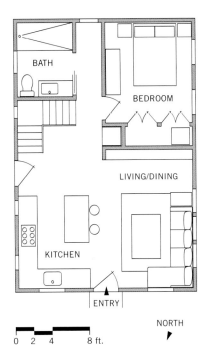

NORTH

0   2   4   8 ft.

SPECS

Bedrooms: 1
Bathrooms: 1
Size: 850 sq. ft.
Location: Kent, Conn.
Designer/builder: Paul and Angela Yagid
Landscape: Richard Schipul, designingeden.com

SEPARATE, TOGETHER

Many homeowners associate comfort with volume. The larger the space, they think, the better it must feel. Often, the most uncomfortable spaces are those that tend to meander on, where there is no order or definitive area to occupy. Even in a small home, you can create a definitive delineation of "rooms" through choices in finish materials, furnishing, and even lighting.

OPPOSITE: A VIEW WITH NO END IN SIGHT. The living room is defined by a wall of built-in cabinetry adjacent to the kitchen, and the natural timbered ceiling in the main hall guides you to the private areas of the home. A window strategically placed at the end of the hall allows your view from the front door to be carried straight through the house and into the trees.

BELOW: A CORNER KITCHEN. Granite-topped counters set flush with the windowsills reduce the visual barriers between the kitchen and the outside patio. Hidden in the beams above, spotlights illuminate the island and in the evening help set the kitchen apart from the other spaces.

LEFT: WINDOWS MAKE THE SPACE. The three tall windows in the main living room flood the space with light and offer abundant views. Their tall head height, combined with the vaulted ceiling, helps enhance the perception of space. The coffee table transforms the room into a dining area that can seat up to ten (see p. 51).

RIGHT: AN AWAY SPACE. Every home, no matter its size, needs a space for personal retreat. The loft is that space in this home, and it serves as a home office, a reading lounge, and even sleeping quarters for visiting grandchildren and guests. As much space as possible beneath the eaves has been captured for seasonal storage.

LET THE DETAILS SHINE

In a small house, a few quality items can really stand out and establish the style of the home. Here, particular attention was given to the things used and experienced most often, which were budgeted for accordingly. It's a good lesson: The things you use and touch on a daily basis should be of the best quality you can afford.

LEFT: A SIMPLE, SUBTLE SOLUTION. The nickel-gap cladding, placement of windows, and lack of upper cabinets at the range wall made conventional tile-backsplash options problematic. The solution was to choose a backsplash that virtually disappeared. It is made of glass that was custom-cut locally and back-painted by ColorKote of Stratford, Conn., to match the Benjamin Moore white on the walls.

BELOW LEFT AND RIGHT: MARBLE, GLASS, AND WOOD. The subway-tiled shower, glass rolling door, and marble-topped vanity provide a clean, contemporary look. The ceiling is clad with original random-width boards above existing beams, adding richness and warmth.

MORE THAN JUST A SET OF STAIRS. The stairs to the loft serve as a focal point as much as functional access. A small window and sconce in the landing illuminate the stairwell, and a built-in bookcase gives additional utility. The railing by View Rail adds a slightly modern touch. The handrail is made of salvaged chestnut from parts of the original interior framing. Every time you ascend to the loft, you're grasping at history.

tage of the light and views they provide. With the living room and kitchen placement positioned at the front of the house, the bedroom and bathroom were located in the opposing rear corners, compressed beneath a rebuilt loft that now serves as a flex space.

The idea of "compression and release" in the context of spatial planning is a hallmark of Frank Lloyd Wright's approach to design. Even in a home as small as this, you can still achieve some of the experience this strategy yields by being mindful of the scale of rooms. Private spaces like the bathroom and bedroom don't need to be large, and certainly don't need vaulted ceilings. Rebuilding the loft to lower the ceiling height in these spaces, and the small hallway bridging the two, helped create a dynamic floor plan. It has the feel of an open plan, but with the functionality of a well-organized and compartmentalized design.

SMALL-HOME SOLUTIONS

There are a few key elements in this home that increase the flexibility of spaces and offer problem-solving solutions for designing and constructing tight, sometimes constricting, areas. These are products you might consider for your next small-home project.

ABOVE LEFT: STACK EFFECT. The Miele Stackable Compact washer and dryer easily tucks into the master-bedroom closet. The dryer is a condensing unit, so traditional venting isn't necessary, which makes placement within a small home much easier.

ABOVE RIGHT: A TIGHT-FITTING FRIDGE. Due to their size, refrigerators are notoriously problematic when designing small kitchens. Fortunately, Liebherr has several options to consider. This unit is only 30 in. wide, 24 in. deep, and 80 in. high and has a robust amount of storage.

With the core spaces defined within the existing footprint, light and views became the focus when discussing how to make the small spaces as inviting and attractive as possible. In a small home, subtle moves have major impact. For instance, a window with a tall head height will always make a room feel larger than it is. Glazed exterior doors or a window placed at the end of a hallway allows your view to extend beyond the walls to the outdoors and makes a space feel expansive. Even a small window in a stairwell landing can create a major impression. Its scale and placement is fun in that it's somewhat unexpected, and the light it provides brings life to an otherwise dark corner. In combination, all these design moves have helped create a home that belies its diminutive size.

It's borderline inaccurate to refer to this project as a remodel. The only original elements are the stone foundation, the frame-and-board sheathing, and the fir flooring. Everything else was replaced or added, including a new well and septic. But whenever walls and ceilings are exposed—or siding is removed—there's an opportunity to improve the efficiency of a home. In this instance, there was the potential to reduce the operating cost of the house, make it far more comfortable than at any other time in its hundred-year history, and reduce its resource consumption without an over-the-top insulation and mechanical package.

The true 2x4 walls were sprayed with open-cell spray foam, and enough rigid foam was added to the exterior to move the dew point outside the wall cavity. While the board sheathing has a much better buffer capacity than modern sheathing when wetting and drying, the walls were still designed to be able to dry to the interior. The ceiling was

A COFFEE TABLE THAT SEATS TEN. The coffee table in the living room is built by Expand Furniture in Vancouver. It lifts and separates to become a table when entertaining guests. Extension leaves are stowed inside when not in use. Here, it's set for six with Nano padded folding chairs, also by Expand Furniture, that take up a mere 13 in. of depth when stacked together.

addressed exclusively from the interior in order to avoid changing the home's aesthetics and to make the most of a finite budget. Polyiso rigid foam was cut to fit between framing members and air-sealed in place to create a hot roof that would yield as much insulating value as possible. Below, the crawl-space was detailed with heavy-duty poly sheeting to reduce moisture migration into the basement and insulated with a combination of closed-cell spray foam and high-density fiberglass batts. A new forced-air system, an on-demand water heater, and an HRV keep the house comfortable and supplied with fresh air. While the home has not been tested or certified by any third-party energy programs, it has been retrofitted to perform well above what the local code demands, providing resiliency and economy.

When people see this home, or experience others like it, they tend to make associations with moments or experiences in either their own lives or in our collective history. They think of a simple life or of a simpler time. They're appropriate thoughts, because a small home forces you to streamline the things in your life. By distilling its design, a small home—and the lifestyle it reinforces—gives you the room for experiences that are more spiritual in nature than they are tangible, and that ultimately tends to feel more fulfilling. Within the frenetic world we live, it's alluring.

William Henry Channing, a philosopher and friend to Henry David Thoreau—whose cabin at Walden is among the most influential small homes in our history—has a quote that describes the ethos of the transcendentalists of the time: "To live content with small means; to seek elegance rather than luxury, and refinement rather than fashion." While my parents are not transcendentalists, this very sentiment is realized in the completion of their new home. It's all that they need at this point in their lives, and it's all that they could want.

BACKYARD COTTAGE

An 800-sq.-ft. backyard cottage exemplifies the benefits of downsizing and reveals a new housing opportunity

BY MATT HUTCHINS

IN SEATTLE, SEVERAL SMALL HOUSES ARE POPPING up, but they are not where you might expect. Modeled on carriage houses of old, these backyard cottages are second houses on the same lots as primary residences. They offer occupants established, walkable neighborhoods, with the public transportation and local businesses sorely lacking in far-flung suburbs.

To keep the cottages in sync with neighborhood character, Seattle's new zoning ordinance is strict: In addition to conforming to typical total lot coverage, setbacks, and off-street parking, a cottage can be no more than 800 net sq. ft., with a 23-ft. height limit. The net-square-footage rule means that the thickness of the walls is not included in the total amount of living space.

Our firm, CAST architecture, was itching to design a house that would satisfy the city's new rules and whatever needs a client might bring to the party. Enter Ken and Marilyn Widner. They had been thinking about downsizing after retirement, and having a new cottage seemed like the perfect solution to update their lifestyle without having to leave their beloved neighborhood. Instead of spending time cleaning the 3,000-sq.-ft. house they raised their family in, they would be able to rent it and spend time traveling.

Their goals didn't stop there. The Widners wanted to keep as much yard as possible for gardening, to build green, to harvest rainwater, and to make space for their vinyl LP collection and mementos collected from a lifetime of travel. The new house also had to be a good neighbor to the turn-of-the-20th-century bungalows lining the street.

We sat down with the site map, subtracted the setbacks, and calculated the available lot coverage. The maximum buildable footprint was 452 sq. ft. With a two-story house, we were in business.

COMPROMISES AND A COMFORTABLE KITCHEN

Not everything magically fits into a smaller footprint. At our first meeting, we sketched out the basics: a two-bedroom house with 1½ baths. Some choices were easy, such as skipping a formal dining room; summertime dining in the garden would take its place. In the entry, we opted for a coatrack instead of a closet. Upstairs, a stackable washer/dryer coupled with a big linen closet eliminated the need for a laundry room. Other decisions were tough; for example, the cottage doesn't have a tub, much to Marilyn's chagrin.

OUTDOOR ROOMS MAKE SMALL HOUSES LARGER. A dining table and chairs extend the living space to the garden. Buried beneath the patio, a 1,500-gal. cistern stores runoff for toilets, laundry, and irrigation. The steeply pitched gable roof echoes those of neighboring houses. Photo taken at A on floor plan.

NO WASTED SPACE

Locating storage, stairs, and the radiant-floor boiler closet on the west wall allowed plenty of windows on the east wall. The kitchen has lots of counter space, but not much floor space, which encourages guests to stay on the dining-table side of the peninsula.

SPECS

Bedrooms: 2
Bathrooms: 1½
Size: 854 sq. ft. gross; 800 sq. ft. net
Cost: $351 per gross sq. ft.
Completed: 2011
Location: Seattle, Wash.
Architect: CAST architecture, Seattle, castarchitecture.com
Builder: Zoltan Farkas

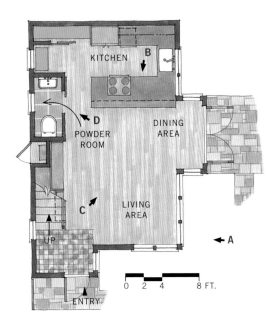

FIRST FLOOR

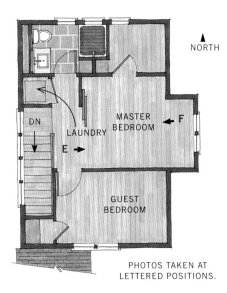

PHOTOS TAKEN AT LETTERED POSITIONS.

SECOND FLOOR

Marilyn does a lot of cooking and baking. She needed a big work counter with space around the stove and ample cabinets, but she didn't need floor area for multiple cooks. We pored through every drawer in her original kitchen to learn what Marilyn needed space for in her new kitchen. Now, Marilyn is never more than a few steps from every dish, spatula, and cookie sheet, and she still has plenty of room for her giant paella pan.

CATHEDRAL CEILINGS AND LONG VIEWS ENERGIZE THE HOUSE

Vaulting a ceiling can make all the difference between drab and dramatic. Upstairs, we vaulted all the ceilings and placed skylights in every room and in the walk-in closet. Seattle's gray winter skies are actually filled with bright, even light—enough to keep the lights off. In the bathroom, the light streaming from above bounces off the azure glass tiles, giving the whole room a sun-kissed Mediterranean feel.

ABOVE: FOCUS ON THE GARDEN. Clustering storage, stairs, and the powder room along the west wall allowed plenty of east-facing windows overlooking the garden. The big peninsula is cooking central, with a bar, space for buffets, dish storage, and glass display. A slightly lower ceiling on the west side of the living room is a subtle suggestion of the path through the house. Photo taken at C on floor plan.

LEFT: NO DOWNSTAIRS PARTITIONS. Long diagonal views from the kitchen to the entry stretch the sense of space. The tansu-style staircase packs a lot of storage into a small space. Like the floor, the tansu unit is made of engineered bamboo. Photo taken at B on floor plan

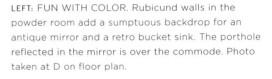

LEFT: FUN WITH COLOR. Rubicund walls in the powder room add a sumptuous backdrop for an antique mirror and a retro bucket sink. The porthole reflected in the mirror is over the commode. Photo taken at D on floor plan.

BELOW LEFT AND RIGHT: INHABIT THE ROOF. The vaulted ceilings and window bump-out in the master bedroom heighten the sense of space. Barn doors close off the room for privacy when guests are in town. Photos taken at E and F on floor plan.

To make the cottage feel big, we ganged the closed functions (storage, cabinets, bathrooms, utilities) and pushed them to the north and west walls, where windows would have been facing neighboring houses. The staircase became a tansu cabinet housing the stereo, LPs, flat-screen TV, books, and mementos. Behind the TV, a boiler for the hydronic radiant floors is accessed from outside. This left a relatively large area with great light on the east and south overlooking the garden. A room with a view will always feel bigger than it is.

A YEAR LATER

The Widners' cottage has been the talk of the neighborhood—not because of its size, but because of how it feels large and cozy at the same time. When we hosted an open house for the public last July, one person commented in disbelief, "800 sq. ft.? It feels like twice that." Having lived in the house for a year now, Ken and Marilyn wouldn't want all that extra space anyway.

FOCUS ON DETAILS

Details breathe life into a house. By having less square footage, the Widners could concentrate on better materials and fixtures. Here are some highlights:

- Custom cherry cabinetry
- Custom metal railings with stainless-steel cable rail
- Premium double-hung windows from Marvin and portholes from Andersen
- Copper gutter and rain chain
- Vertical-grain Douglas-fir trim and doors
- Glass tile in the master bath
- An antique mirror and retro bucket sink from Alape in the powder room
- A custom pot rack made of the rock screen used by quarries to separate gravel
- A laminated bamboo handrail that resembles custom inlay, which is simply two layers of Plyboo
- Radiant floors (concrete downstairs, Warmboard upstairs)

PIVOT-POINT SOLUTION

Site restrictions and environmental concerns required a "bend" at the center of the house, which keeps the scale in check

BY KILEY JACQUES

THE FORM OF THIS HOUSE IS A RESPONSE TO THE environmental conditions, which included required buffers from nearby wetlands, a natural stream, and an existing well. Building on the already disturbed site of an existing mobile home reduced additional impact on the site while leaving a portion of the seven acres relatively untouched.

The "bend" at the center of the house is a direct result of these restrictions. This pivot point created a few advantageous design opportunities—the biggest of which was keeping the scale in check. The bulk of the building's length visually disappears when viewed from the majority of exterior angles. The one-story eastern side of the house has a modest profile and is broken up with two lower "sheds" sided in clear-finished cedar. Seen broadside from farther away, the western side of the house is appropriately stately. The orientation allows the high window in the south gable to bring light deep into the kitchen.

Sustainability measures included advanced framing methods to minimize wood and maximize insulation. The framing is stacked to create a direct load path from roof to foundation. In the center section, the framing pivots around the main entry and stair connecting all three floors.

As the homeowners intend to age in place, the linear main-floor plan keeps all essential elements on one level. From the entry, the space opens out and down, following the topography. The distant view is framed by two mature cedar trees—another decision made to tie the home to its site.

Designer: Harrison Architects, harrisonarchitects.com
Builder: Phoenix Construction, myphoenixconstructioninc.com
Location: Woodinville, Wash.
Photos: Rob Harrison, courtesy of Harrison Architects

"I took a 'Design with Nature' approach to the site. By layering the various constraints, you end up focusing in on the area that makes the most sense to build on."

—Rob Harrison, Harrison Architects

A COTTAGE ON MARTHA'S VINEYARD

Reworking the floor plan makes the home feel more spacious

BY KILEY JACQUES

THE CURRENT HOMEOWNER GREW UP IN THIS classic agrarian cottage on Martha's Vineyard. When she inherited the property, she decided to convert what had become a two-family house back to a single-family residence, similar to the one she remembered. The challenge was to make the 1,200-sq.-ft. home feel bigger than it is. LDa Architecture & Interiors's design plan eliminated redundant spaces to create a cohesive single-family layout. To start, they gutted compartmentalized spaces to make living areas feel roomier. Cased openings allow common areas to overlap while remaining distinct, and vaulted ceilings in the kitchen and porch add volume. They also changed the circulation; rather than cutting through rooms, occupants now walk along the edges, which makes floors look wider. To enhance natural light, dormers were added to the second floor, and a new porch in the knuckle of the two forms expands the kitchen into an outdoor dining area. Simple materials and light paint colors keep the small spaces from feeling cramped.

Designer: LDa Architecture & Interiors,
        lda-architects.com
Builder: 41 Degrees North Construction
Location: Martha's Vineyard, Mass.
Photos: Sean Litchfield Photography

HOW TO LIVE WELL WITH LESS

At 1,000 sq. ft. smaller than the average house, this compact home is comfortable, practical, and attainable

BY ANNE CALLENDER

I MET DAVE AND LIBBY AT A WEDDING IN THE FALL of 2010. My husband and I had just moved into their neighborhood as they were putting their three-story Victorian home on the market in order to move to a small house on Munjoy Hill in Portland, Maine. As we spoke about the large remodeling project we were undertaking, they spoke of their readiness to leave behind the 3,200-sq.-ft. home where they had raised their three daughters. The house was too big for them now, and the maintenance demands were too great. They travel a lot, and they were at a point in their lives where they could redefine how they wanted to live. Like a lot of empty-nesters, they were eager to downsize to a much smaller home and to unload a good portion of their material possessions in the process.

AN OLD HOUSE IN AN EVOLVING NEIGHBORHOOD

Dave and Libby had owned the small house on Munjoy Hill for several years and used it as a rental property. Located in a densely built residential neighborhood established by Italian immigrants, it sits two blocks from Casco Bay and the Eastern Promenade, a beautiful city park designed by the Olmsted Brothers. Munjoy Hill's aging housing stock, harbor views, fabulous park, and proximity to downtown have made this area the hottest part of town and a prime spot for aggressive rehabs.

Dave and Libby's house was built in 1879, and when they considered moving there full-time, they were forced to assess its condition carefully. Having withstood the coastal Maine environment for well over a hundred years, the house was quickly approaching the end of its useful life. There was a fair amount of rot, the foundation was out of square, the basement was frequently wet, and all of the major elements—mechanicals, windows, roof, siding—needed to be replaced. Dave and Libby realized one day that not a single original detail was left in the house. They quickly replaced their thoughts of a restoration with an acknowledgment that what little could be saved wasn't worth saving and that starting over would be the best and most practical option.

PRIME SITING ON A SMALL LOT

Dave and Libby's lot is only 36 ft. wide and 105 ft. deep, and it lies on a decent slope. The existing house was built to the rear of the lot and close to the west and north lot lines. Fortunately, the neighboring houses were situated close to the street. Dave and Libby wanted to build on the footprint of the old house, and its location offered some nice advantages: Dave and Libby wouldn't be looking directly into the neighbors' windows,

DOWNSIZING WITHOUT SACRIFICING. For empty-
nesters and baby boomers heading toward retirement, this compact 1,600-sq.-ft. home shows that
downsizing doesn't have to come with sacrifices in
style, comfort, and good living.

PRACTICALLY PLANNED

The new stair tower blocks the backyard and the deck from public view, and it helps to streamline the arrangement of the main living spaces. The front-to-back sequence of living room, dining room, and kitchen is typical of shotgun-style homes or industrial lofts. The lack of interior walls allows the spaces to be defined by art and furnishings, giving the owners ongoing flexibility.

SPECS

Bedrooms: 2, plus flex office space
Bathrooms: 1½
Size: 1,600 sq. ft.
Cost: $280 per sq. ft., including custom furnishings
Completed: 2012
Location: Portland, Maine
Architect: Anne Callender, whipplecallender.com
Builder: Rick Romano, papiandromanobuilders.com

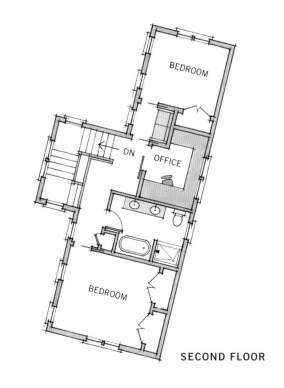

SECOND FLOOR

NORTH ▲

0 2 4   8 ft.

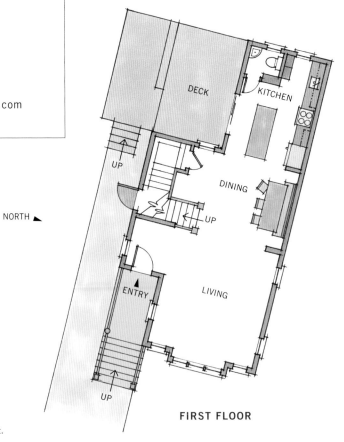

FIRST FLOOR

RESTRAINED LIVING. The monochromatic color scheme inside—all of the walls, cabinetry, trim, and ceilings are painted the same linen white—gives the house a more contemporary, gallery feel and highlights its few playfully colored furnishings and plentiful art.

but onto their backyards. The neighbors' homes wouldn't shade Dave and Libby's house, so the couple would have greater access to daylight. Also, if we built on the existing footprint, the zoning board would allow us to increase the height by one story and to add on to the south side of the house.

A TRADITIONAL HOME WITH CONTEMPORARY DETAILS

The houses surrounding the property are mostly folk Victorians. Dave and Libby wanted to preserve the neighborhood aesthetic on the exterior; on the interior, however, they wanted a contemporary, open plan.

The house's traditional qualities are established with its simple gable roof facing the street, its wide trim boards, and its first-floor box-bay window. The side porch entry, which was a key element on the original house, was replicated on the new house. This allowed for the main volume of the living space to be uninterrupted and open from the front of the house to the back.

The placement of the interior stairs was no less critical. In dense neighborhoods, the daylight on a

9 WAYS TO MAKE THE MOST OF SMALL SPACES

1 Designing with 9-ft. ceilings adds volume to narrow floor plans.

2 Placing stairs strategically provides daylight access and views.

3 Flexible spaces allow homeowners to react to changing lifestyle demands.

4 See-through items—such as a kitchen island or a transom—provide extended views through small spaces.

5 Open, shotgun-style floor plans offer shared views and daylight, and they allow defined living spaces to expand as needed.

6 Big-house features—such as multiple bedrooms, bathrooms, and office space— ensure living without compromise.

7 Adequate storage space relieves the burden on main living areas, enabling them to remain open and free of clutter.

8 Providing access to outdoor living areas in narrow floor plans increases the perception of space and improves comfort.

9 Monochromatic finishes make small spaces feel larger and contiguous by blurring their boundaries.

"This home has all the elements that make up much larger homes. Nothing about this design demands sacrifice."

home's second floor is usually better than on the first floor because of shading from the abutting properties and trees. Placing the interior stair on the south side of the house and wrapping the well with glass allowed daylight to flood both floors. In addition to light access, the height of the stairwell adds volume and spaciousness to what could have been a long, narrow, and cramped first-floor living space.

COMPACT, BUT EXPANSIVE AND FLEXIBLE

The small house was designed to feel as open and large as possible. The 9-ft. ceilings certainly help in that effort, but it's in the arrangement of spaces that a sense of expansiveness and flexibility is achieved.

The main floor is arranged shotgun style, with the living room, dining room, and kitchen sharing a contiguous space from front to back. The bathroom sits in one corner at the back of the house, and the kitchen in the other. The kitchen cabinetry abuts the north wall in order to preserve direct access to sunlight from the south.

Immediately outside the kitchen, we built a deck that is accessed through large sliding patio doors. This visual connection from the kitchen to the yard makes a 12-ft.-wide space expand well beyond the interior walls. Libby designed the kitchen island with builder Rick Romano, who also built the custom cabinets. It has a band of drawers and is open below, which adds to the sense of space

OPPOSITE: THE LADIES" AND THEIR STAIR. The owners, parents of three daughters, felt that most all stock newel posts had a masculine look. These custom newel posts built by Rick Romano are designed to suggest a more feminine figure. The owners call them "the ladies." The stairway serves as an important source of daylight to the first and second floors.

RIGHT: ONE SPACE, TWO ROLES. A laundry room is carved out of the hallway between the stair's top landing area and the guest room. Adding such functionality to circulation areas makes the most of limited square footage.

and openness. It's also placed atop casters, which allow its role to change from a prep area to a serving buffet simply by altering its location within the large living space.

There are no interior walls on the first floor, except for two small fin walls that define the end of the kitchen and the extent of the dining area. These walls are also used as the plumbing chases to the second-floor bathroom and laundry room.

Since the house is occupied by two empty-nesters most of the time, even the second floor was conceived as an open space. The two bedrooms are located at opposite ends of the house, book-ending a bath, office, and laundry space. A sliding barn door for the office lets the space double as a guest room. Its opening can be reframed to create another bedroom, should future owners need one. A laundry room and hallway were combined in a niche between the stair landing and the guest bedroom. Pocket doors close it off from sight and sound as needed.

In another effort to add flexibility and functionality to the home, we placed a side door onto a lower landing to the basement. This gives Dave and Libby exterior access to the basement for dirty or oversize items such as shovels, snow tires, and the like. Because we made the effort to create a dry basement, Dave and Libby have plenty of space for storage. Moreover, the windows allow for it to be finished comfortably in the future if a family with children moves in and needs additional living or play space.

SMALL IS RELATIVE

This home has all the elements that make up much larger homes: two bedrooms, a home office, one and a half baths, a spacious kitchen, and a generous living area. Finishes and materials were selected for their ease of maintenance. Nothing about this design demands sacrifice. There are rooms to retreat to if anyone needs privacy. Dave and Libby still can host parties for 50 to 60 people, and with the house so open and comfortable, party guests actually move out of the kitchen.

DOWNTOWN
DESIGN

A compact infill home is at the forefront of progressive urban development

BY JAMES TUER

LIVING IN THE CITY DOESN'T HAVE TO REQUIRE A compromise in the quality of living, as some rural and suburban dwellers assume. You don't have to forfeit a sense of privacy, give up a love of nature, or be forced to drive far outside city limits to find true refuge. When designed well, a home in a dense city neighborhood can provide quiet and personal space while keeping its owners thoroughly connected to the pulse of the urban landscape.

When my Vancouver, B.C., clients, a couple of empty-nesters who faced the possibility of boomerang kids, approached me for help in designing a new home, I saw an opportunity to utilize my backgrounds in urban planning and residential architecture. I wanted to design a modern home that would make use of the most-progressive zoning laws, passive-design strategies, and high-performance construction techniques in order to deliver my clients the home they'd always dreamed of. But I also recognized this as an opportunity to design a home that would challenge some of the notions about who lives in the city and how they live.

ONE LOT, TWO HOMES

My clients' vision for their new home was pretty simple: Create a modern, efficient home within 1,600 sq. ft. They were also interested in building a laneway home, what some people refer to as an accessory dwelling unit (ADU) or a backyard cottage (see "Building out back," p. 77).

Their property occupies a small corner lot in the hip Kitsilano neighborhood—the Haight-Ashbury of 1960s Vancouver. I often look at a corner lot as a gift, since it allows me to design a building that is much more than just a facade facing a street. Making this site even more special are the trees that line the intersecting streets, which are over 100 years old. Because this corner lot was on a "short" block, though, we would have to work within a site of only 80 ft. by 40 ft.—pretty tight, given my clients' wish list.

Modern urban homes on such small lots tend to be focused inward, and if they open up to the city, it's most often only on the upper floors through moderate-size windows. I rethought this paradigm with my approach to the site and the house, and the result was a house that's more open to its surroundings. For instance, an oversize corner window provides a wide view of the street from the living room. The small front-yard landscape terrace and gabion wall, softened by lush plantings, create a buffer for privacy. Both the main house and the laneway cottage open up to the back garden through lots of glass. Clerestory windows and a raised corner

TIMELESS MODERN COMPACT INFILL. Modern in style and construction, this infill home and laneway cottage are at the forefront of progressive urban development and forward-thinking home building.

CARVING PRIVACY OUT OF AN URBAN LOT

The goal in designing the two houses on this small lot
was to make the city go away. This was accomplished with
three key strategies: First, placing the house on grade
creates a level garden layout where any plants can double
as screens. Second, gabion walls and board-formed walls
are used to define a series of outdoor rooms and to create
a boundary between the streets. Finally, designing the
footprint of the laneway cottage as a trapezoid helps to
make the small courtyard feel more secluded—more like
a country garden than an urban patio.

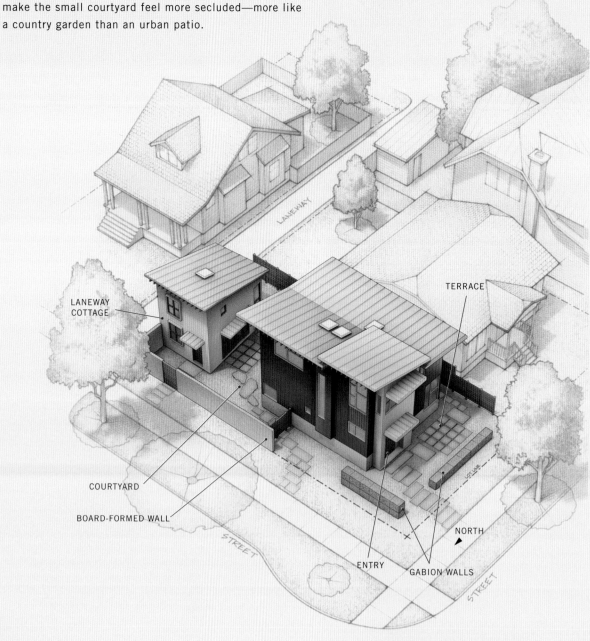

LANEWAY

LANEWAY
COTTAGE

TERRACE

COURTYARD

BOARD-FORMED WALL

LOT LINE

STREET

NORTH

ENTRY

GABION WALLS

STREET

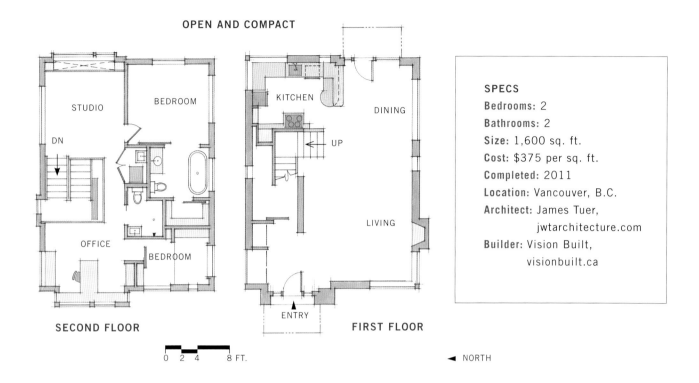

OPEN AND COMPACT

STUDIO

BEDROOM

DN

OFFICE

BEDROOM

SECOND FLOOR

KITCHEN

DINING

UP

LIVING

ENTRY

FIRST FLOOR

0   2   4   8 FT.

◄ NORTH

SPECS
Bedrooms: 2
Bathrooms: 2
Size: 1,600 sq. ft.
Cost: $375 per sq. ft.
Completed: 2011
Location: Vancouver, B.C.
Architect: James Tuer,
        jwtarchitecture.com
Builder: Vision Built,
        visionbuilt.ca

window in the main house's kitchen draw light and views of the mature trees along the north side, and the corner window permits views over the concrete wall that straddles the property line. At the same time, the wall and the landscaping soften the noise of the street and give an illusion of being removed from it.

REGIONAL STYLE

Broad overhangs, access to light and views, and a shed-style roof that opens up to the north contribute to a style of architecture that feels at home in this Pacific Northwest climate. Urban features include standing-seam aluminum siding and splashes of bright colors, which help define the entryways and some of the feature windows.

These design elements helped us achieve the timeless modern look the owners most desired. They wanted the house to be defined as much by its natural surroundings—the view of the distant mountains and the native plantings within the garden—as they did by the many Craftsman-style cottages in the area. As a gesture to the Craftsman

style, I chose to expose the rafter tails and to use Douglas fir on the underside of the roofs. Rather than have simple modern picture windows, each window is unique and is defined by its mullion patterns. This is also a nod to more traditional architecture found in the neighborhood.

While the main house and the laneway cottage have similar attributes, they're not identical twins. The two buildings share one common element: the concrete landscape wall that traverses the property line. A simple aluminum gate breaks the wall and becomes the formal arrival point for the occupants of the smaller laneway cottage. The laneway cottage is sided with a 1x4 tongue-and-groove cedar siding painted light gray. The product is referred to as "fine line" because of a thin ¼-in. reveal sawn into each board to create a subtle shadow line. We also reversed the color scheme. The windows are orange rather than yellow as on the main house, and the accent panels are yellow rather than orange. This is a simple yet effective way of making the two houses feel like they are of the same family while retaining their own, independent identities.

ABOVE: LIVING LIGHT. The 11-ft.-tall main-floor living space is grounded by polished-concrete floors and is daylit with large windows and doors that have been installed with reveals around their jambs, instead of trim, to reinforce the modern aesthetic.

LEFT: OPEN ABOVE AND BELOW. The kitchen is partially defined by a tiered peninsula set under two matte-black Sentry pendant lights. Open shelves hang above a stainless-steel countertop and Kindred undermount sink. Light streams through corner windows and through a window above that illuminates the kitchen and the studio.

BUILT-IN ENERGY SAVINGS

This new home was designed with several strategies to naturally condition interior spaces and reduce energy usage and costs. The carefully detailed feature stairway to the second floor plays a major role in the home's passive performance.

PASSIVE VENTILATION
Operable windows facilitate cross ventilation. Rooftop skylights provide natural ventilation via the stack effect, a cyclical flow of air driven by differences in air temperature and density.

THERMAL MASS
Solar energy heats the concrete surfaces and is radiated during low-light hours to help warm the house in cooler months. In warmer months, opening windows at night allows cool air to chill the concrete. If windows are kept shut during the day, the concrete will wick warmth out of the indoor air and help keep interior spaces comfortable.

PASSIVE SOLAR
Roof overhangs are optimized to shade interior spaces during the summer and to allow sunlight to penetrate deep into the house when the winter sun is lower in the sky. Large windows on eastern and southern facades increase the amount of daylight entering the home. They also increase the amount of solar energy, which is stored in the interior concrete components.

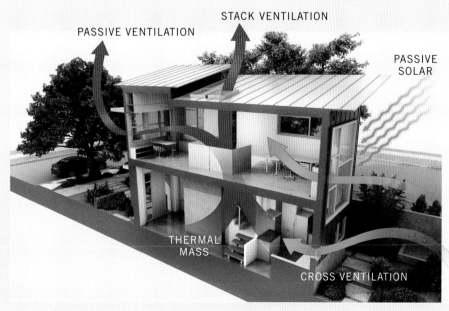

BUILT TO LAST. Standing-seam aluminum siding wraps the main house and ensures a long-lasting, weather-tight envelope while clearly defining the home's modern style.

A PASSIVE APPROACH TO SYSTEMS

For those who aren't familiar with the Pacific Northwest, I often compare Vancouver's climate to North Carolina's. When doing so, however, I note two main differences: We have more rain and less sunshine in the winter and a drier heat in the summer, which is prone to settle over the city in long stretches. Many homeowners here want air-conditioning, but my clients wanted the house to ventilate and cool naturally. Strategically placed windows provide ventilation, and lots of exposed concrete offers thermal mass to assist in space conditioning.

Another important consideration was to ensure that large expanses of glass did not act as solar collectors and overheat the house in the summer. Fortunately, the trees that shade both floors keep the house cool. In the winter, when the trees drop their leaves, the sun reaches deep into the house and stores its energy in the exposed concrete, helping to warm the space during low-light hours.

A THICK, DURABLE SHELL

One of my clients' primary goals was to create a home that was durable and long lasting. The strategy, then, led to one of those design elements that set out to solve one problem and ended up helping to meet a second set of design goals. In order to increase the house's resilience and keep its main floor at grade, we decided to raise the stemwalls roughly 4 ft. out of the ground and to clad the walls above them with standing-seam aluminum siding. This required us to build a double-stud wall on the main level—one 2x6 wall atop the stemwall and another 2x6 wall atop the slab—to meet the building code's energy standards and to allow us to finish the interior with drywall down to the slab. On the second floor, we stayed with a thick-wall approach by using 2x10 plates and staggered 2x4 studs. Filling the 12-in. and 10-in. cavities with open-cell spray foam yielded airtight walls over R-30.

Another area we paid careful attention to was the intersection of the slab and the stemwall. Concrete is a naturally conductive material, and we wanted to ensure that we would not lose heat through the assembly. The slab "floats" on 4 in. of rigid insulation, and a 2x4 strip of rigid insulation lies between the slab and the stemwall. This thermal break is also important because the slab is the medium for our radiant-heat system, and we certainly did not want that heat escaping into the stemwall, which we left exposed on the exterior.

The well-insulated, airtight home is ventilated naturally, but a heat-recovery ventilator efficiently keeps a steady supply of fresh air circulating. In the city of Vancouver, progressive in many ways, heat-recovery ventilators are mandated by city codes.

EMBRACE THE CITY

The one thing about cities is that they are always changing. Embracing that change can be incredibly rewarding. For those looking to move into the city or to design an urban home, I have a few words of advice.

BUILDING OUT BACK

Laneway housing is a form of building that treats laneways as streets and allows homeowners to build small cottages in their backyards. More than 10-year-old practice in Vancouver, B.C., laneway housing is slowly taking root in municipalities throughout Canada and the United States.

In concept, by allowing laneway cottages, a municipality can double the number of houses that can be built in a neighborhood. This provides a diversity of housing options within a single-family neighborhood, with the laneway cottages tending to cater to people who may not fit into the typical single-family-house demographic. This in turn creates a more interesting place to live. Kids or aging parents can take

advantage of housing that is readily multigenerational and of the social benefits that this concept brings with it—a greater connection to urban services and infrastructure and a significant reduction in transportation costs and carbon footprints.

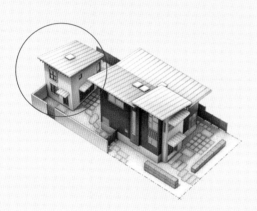

First, do not worry about maximizing building floor areas and building heights. Land is expensive in many cities, but you are still far better off building smaller and smarter than worrying about the future resale value of the house.

Second, bring nature into the city. Don't concern yourself with precisely mirroring the neighborhood. If you are inspired by the ocean or the mountains or the desert, bring a little of that inspiration into your landscape design. This project was

partially influenced by the mountains, and so we brought in large granite boulders to grace the lot.

Finally, just because you are in the city doesn't mean you can't build efficiently. Maximizing natural daylight through clever placement of windows is easy. Also, if your site allows it, consider alternative solutions to mechanical systems. It's OK if your home looks and functions a bit differently than those of your neighbors.

SMALL-HOME HARMONY

Tight space restrictions, unique cultural requirements, and the desire to age in place informed this compact, efficient design

BY MATT COFFEY

KEN AND FRAN WATSON ENJOY THEIR TWO-STORY vacation home for its capacity to host friends and family, but it is far from the house they imagined for their retirement years. Wishing to build a second residence on their half-acre lot nestled in the heart of West Chop Woods, the couple approached South Mountain Company for our help.

Although zoning allowed for an additional structure, it could not exceed 600 sq. ft. of interior space, so an efficient floor plan was key. The Watsons also had a list of must-haves, which included room for a grand piano, discreet storage for sheet music, and a covered porch. The house had to be comfortable for two people, with space for an occasional guest; it needed to function well acoustically; and it had to feel private, have lots of daylight, and be easy to maintain.

LAYING OUT THE FLOOR PLAN

We began our floor-plan design by asking how compact we could make the bedroom and the bathroom in order to assign more square footage to the public space. Fran and Ken were comfortable with the idea of very modest accommodations and small closets, which allowed us to stretch the west wing to a comfortable size.

Privacy was a leading consideration, too. Because there is less than 60 ft. between the main house and the neighbor's house, we pivoted the west wing 15° to the north. This "kink" in the floor plan opened the entry and shifted perspective from the living space toward the adjacent woods. We concentrated the glazing on the side facing away from the main house, and the modest entry is fully glazed from floor to ceiling to feel open and inviting. As a result of these efforts, when one is in the new house, nearby buildings are largely obscured from view.

SOLVING THE PIANO PUZZLE

The grand piano was the bear in the room. We wanted to position it out of the way, yet make it a focal point. And it was important that the person playing it wouldn't feel cramped. To accomplish this, we bumped the west gable end out 3 ft. This subtle shift reallocated space from where it wasn't needed (a small porch entry door) to where it was (the piano niche). We terminated the southern glazing at this juncture to create a solid exterior wall against which the outswinging door could latch. Sheet music would be stored beneath the large window looking onto the porch, whose sill would extend 20 in. and serve as the top of a custom cypress cabinet with simple bypassing doors.

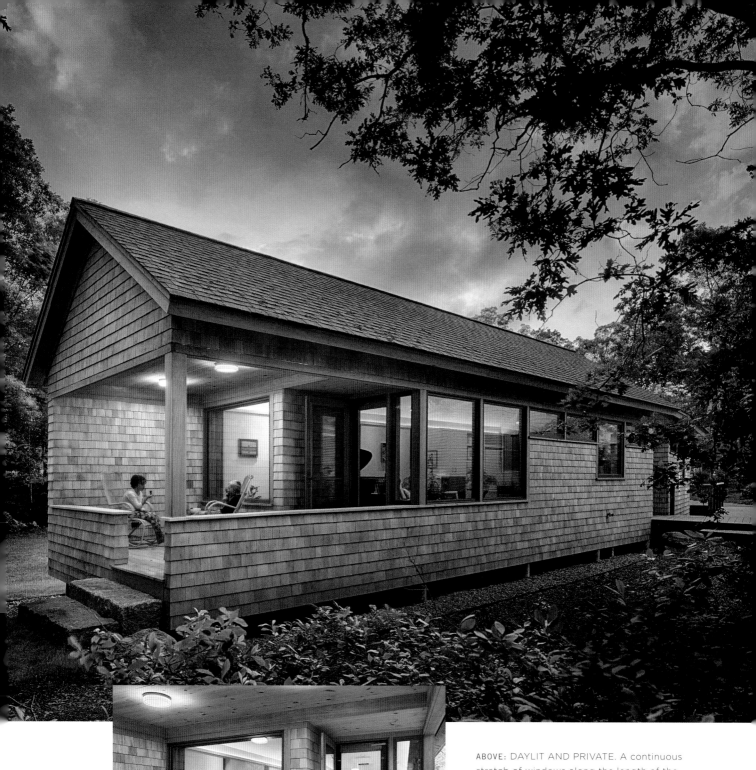

ABOVE: DAYLIT AND PRIVATE. A continuous stretch of windows along the length of the building brings light deep into the 14-ft.-wide interior, and narrow vertical windows are integrated into the 10-in.-thick north walls to balance views with privacy.

LEFT: NOTEWORTHY WOOD. The cypress trim and select millwork are made of old-growth timber harvested from river bottoms in Florida and Georgia. Reclaimed birch sinker logs from a lake in Vermont were used for the flooring.

CONSTRUCTION INNOVATIONS

A site analysis revealed that the back side of the property would be the ideal location for the new house, despite the homeowners' initial plan to build into the hillside at the front. We realized that if we used a pier foundation, we could abut the septic system and the leaching fields, optimizing the remaining buildable strip of land. The septic code dictates that basements and crawlspaces be a minimum of 20 ft. away from a leaching field. Slab-on-grade foundations can be 10 ft. away. If you build on piers, you can build adjacent to a septic system as long as the piers do not disturb or undermine the system, access from above is maintained, and it is permitted by the local building department and board of health.

FIGURING OUT THE FLOOR FRAME

Because we were building on piers just 18 in. off the gravel bed, we were faced with the problem of how to insulate and seal the raised-floor system. We had originally planned to build the floor frame upside down on sawhorses—skinning it with rigid foam and pressure-treated plywood for an airtight layer—and then use a crane to flip it over. Instead, we built a skeletal 2x4 floor frame—just enough of a frame to allow us to put down the first layer of PT plywood and the rigid foam. Working from above, we taped the rigid-foam layer in the floor assembly; the plywood below it was not taped because it was outside of the air barrier. We then built a more conventional 2x12 floor frame on top of that. The subfloor above was taped to keep water out of the assembly during construction, but it was not meant to be an air barrier, so when we pulled up the lightly tacked strips of subfloor to insulate the floor cavity, we did not retape those seams. We had the air-sealing we wanted, and the construction sequence didn't require a crane. Moreover, we didn't have to think in reverse to lay out the plumbing and ductwork.

REGULATING THE WATER LINES

To get water into the house, we wanted to maintain above-freezing temperatures in the water supply line without electric-resistance heat tape, so we decided to build a custom conduit. The town-supplied water comes up from 4 ft. below grade, and right where it turns to enter the building we built a custom-insulated double-wall PVC conduit. The ground temperature and the ambient indoor-air temperature thermally regulate the conduit, which is essentially borrowing 55°F from the ground plus warmth from inside the house.

A SHEATHING LESSON

The roof-truss assembly was another component we developed along the way. Because of its low-environmental impact, we wanted to use dense-pack cellulose insulation wherever possible. Putting the air barrier on the roof interior and transitioning it to the exterior at the wall enabled us to do a vented roof and to use all cellulose.

Above the top plate, where we were transitioning the air barrier from inside to outside, we had to tape every seam. There were a lot of nooks and crannies to seal, and this had to be done perfectly or there would be the possibility of a breach. Next time, a better option might be to use eaveless trusses and to run the air-barrier sheathing right up to the roof sheathing. Then we could add a second layer of 2x4s or 2x6s above that, run those out, and add sheathing above that structure. In other words, we would frame a cold roof, using that whole second layer of framing and sheathing as a vented assembly.

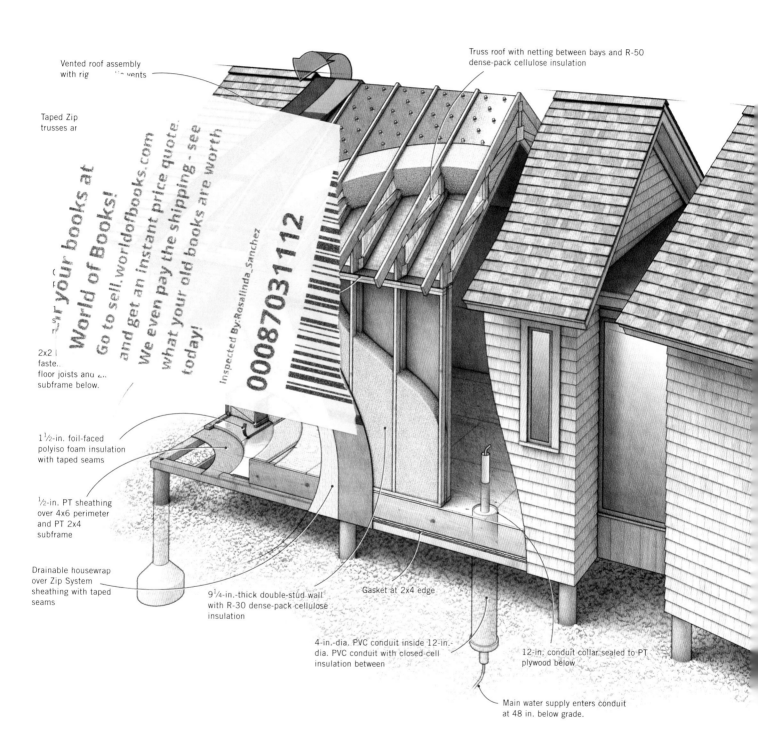

Vented roof assembly with rig___ ___ vents

Taped Zip trusses ar___

2x2 ___ faste__ floor joists and 2___ subframe below.

1 1/2-in. foil-faced polyiso foam insulation with taped seams

1/2-in. PT sheathing over 4x6 perimeter and PT 2x4 subframe

Drainable housewrap over Zip System sheathing with taped seams

9 1/4-in.-thick double-stud wall with R-30 dense-pack cellulose insulation

Truss roof with netting between bays and R-50 dense-pack cellulose insulation

Gasket at 2x4 edge

4-in.-dia. PVC conduit inside 12-in.-dia. PVC conduit with closed-cell insulation between

12-in. conduit collar sealed to PT plywood below

Main water supply enters conduit at 48 in. below grade.

DESIGN FOR AGING IN PLACE

People are increasingly interested in planning their homes around possible future needs. To address that, we developed a three-tiered checklist for aging in place. It has become part of our design process and is now presented to every client.

Each level represents an increase in cost and complexity. We try to incorporate all of the Level 1 provisions (shown below) in every project. We offer Level 2 and Level 3 options to give clients choices if they want to take visitability and accessibility to a higher standard.

ABSOLUTES FOR VISITABILITY
- At least one bath on first floor
- At least one zero-clearance threshold entry
- 32-in. clearance for doors at all visitable spaces

SITE AND ENTRANCE
- No-step route to be 1-in-12 slope; pathway slope of 1-in-20 minimum preferred
- Accessible entry-door threshold to be 1 in. maximum, with bevels above finished floor surface on both sides
- Weather protection from elements to fully cover accessible entry door

INTERIOR CIRCULATION TO VISITABLE SPACES
- Readily visitable spaces via a no-step route to include a full bathroom, bedroom, kitchen, and dining and living space
- Cased openings to be 32 in. wide minimum (34 in. minimum for door slab)
- Level changes in circulation route to visitable spaces via a ramp to be less than 1-in-12 slope
- Minimum 38 in. wide (finished) halls to serve visitable spaces

BEDROOM
- First-floor bedroom (or future bedroom) with 36 in. minimum clearance on one side of bed preferred

HALF-BATHROOM
- Minimum ¾-in. plywood walls or adequate blocking for grab bars at toilet and shower in visitable bathroom at 33 in. to 36 in. above finished floor (2x12 blocking needed for fiberglass units)

FLOORS
- Maximum ½-in. thresholds between floor surfaces in accessible spaces

SWITCHES AND CONTROLS
- Electrical switches to be centered 48 in. maximum above floor
- Thermostats at 48 in. maximum or remote controlled

FIXTURES AND HARDWARE
- Lever handles on doors

TAKING THE LONG VIEW

For comfortable aging in place, we kept everything on one level. The transition from the driveway to the boardwalk and all the way through the house to the back porch is flush—that includes the finished deck, terrace, outdoor shower, and entry.

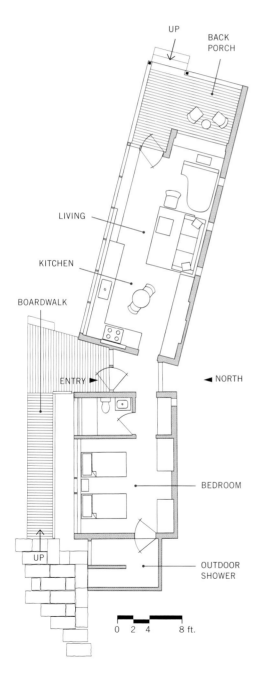

UP

BACK PORCH

LIVING

KITCHEN

BOARDWALK

ENTRY ▶

◀ NORTH

BEDROOM

UP

OUTDOOR SHOWER

0 2 4   8 ft.

SPECS
Bedrooms: 1
Bathrooms: 1
Size: 715 sq. ft.
Completed: 2018
Location: Vineyard Haven, Mass.
Architect/builder: South Mountain Company, www.southmountain.com

LEFT AND RIGHT: BUILT FOR SOUND. The piano sits beneath a 12-ft. ceiling and beside the porch door, which was brought into the conditioned space rather than made flush with the window to optimize the acoustics and save square footage.

To get the acoustics right, we worked with Doug Sturz from Acentech. Our initial schematics divided the house into two volumes with shed roofs, but in order to get the volumetric requirements for high-quality acoustics, Doug suggested a minimum ceiling height of 12 ft. He also explained the need for a mix of solid walls (which could be softened with a tapestry or acoustical panels) and hard surfaces (such as windows) off of which the sound

could travel. An open shelf above the porch entry door would add volume without increasing square footage. In lieu of a cost-prohibitive, acoustically optimized ceiling, we opted for a smooth plaster finish. The homeowners knew from experience that small changes in the room, such as a piece of additional furniture or a wall hanging, can affect acoustics. In the process of moving in, they intentionally utilized space to "fine tune" their home.

We recently visited Ken and Fran and found them settled right in. Ken had set up recording equipment by the piano. After performing his latest composition, he shared this sentiment with us: "We have such appreciation and respect for the design, engineering, detail, uplifting spirit, and harmony of our home. We will age happily because we live in this superbly planned and impressively built home."

TRADITION ON A TIGHT LOT

The design team made sure this new home maximized the site while fitting in with the historical character of its neighborhood

BY JANICE ROHLF

ORIGINALLY LOOKING TO PURCHASE A HISTORICAL home close to downtown Saratoga Springs, N.Y., the owners, upon finding a previously developed lot in a prime location with good walkability, opted instead for a new build. At first unsure of the feasibility of constructing a home, a garage, and a pool on the narrow site, they were ultimately convinced by Balzer & Tuck's design, which not only maximizes the utility of the narrow lot but also references the character of the neighborhood, thus achieving two important goals. With the main residence positioned at the southeast corner of the parcel, there is room for a driveway and detached garage along the north. This allowed a sizable sun-filled rear yard with a private pool and a granite firepit. To achieve an elegant main house from the combination of simple forms and clean lines, the architect drew inspiration from traditional farmhouses of the Northeast. Moreover, the character and style of the owners can be seen throughout the property, from the steeply sloped gable dormer to the kitchen island built of salvaged doors. The heart of the home is an open living and dining space flanked by a large chef's kitchen that overlooks the rear yard. The vaulted screen porch anchors the primary circulation core of the home, with a wood-burning fireplace clad in reclaimed brick that further reinforces this home's connection with its historical environs.

Architect: Balzer & Tuck, balzertuck.com
Builder: Teakwood Builders, teakwoodbuilders.com
Location: Saratoga Springs, N.Y.
Photos: Scott Bergmann Photography

A PROTOTYPE NET-ZERO COTTAGE HOME

Green-building strategies and low-carbon materials define the design of a cluster of energy-efficient, solar-powered homes

BY KILEY JACQUES

THIS IS THE THIRD OF FIVE HOUSES BY ARCHITECT Emily Mottram and builder Patrice Cappelletti. Part of "a little solar community," it is meant to be a prototype for net-zero neighborhood development. The goal was to create comfortable, durable, efficient homes using green-building strategies and nontoxic, low-carbon materials. For top performance, they went with double-stud walls filled with cellulose, and the HVAC systems include ERVs, ductless minisplits, and small woodstoves with outdoor-air intakes ducted directly to the fireboxes. All of the houses run on solar power.

The 2,000-sq.-ft. three-bedroom, two-and-a-half-bath home pictured here includes reclaimed timber beams, recycled bricks for the mudroom flooring, reglazed metal windows from a decommissioned factory, and a slate farmhouse sink, which was sent back to the original local manufacturer for refurbishment. All are intended to give the new home old character.

To tie the structure to its natural surroundings, the team lowered the window sills to 13 in., which helps to draw the eye through the house and beyond; it also creates the illusion of a larger volume. Similarly, scissor trusses on the second floor allow for vaulted ceilings that visually extend the interiors outward, while keeping the home's overall height in check. In the same vein, old barnwood warms and scales down the first-floor bedroom suite.

The local vernacular is seen in the board-and-batten porch—designed for passive shading and optimal winter light—as well as the upper wood-clapboard siding with wide-board trim. This small assembly of houses is both at ease in its northern Maine setting, and built to perform in that bitter-cold climate.

"The goal was to take a property that had been ravaged by timber harvesting and turn it into a community of like-minded individuals with houses that tread lightly, connect to the surroundings, and are healthy for their occupants."

—Emily Mottram, architect

Designer: Mottram Architecture, mottramarch.com
Builder: Live Solar Maine, livesolarmaine.com
Location: Cumberland, Maine
Photos: Michael D. Wilson

A HOUSE ON THE HUDSON

Site constraints and a desire to optimize the view drove the design of this subtle small home

BY PHILIP IVORY

MY WIFE AND I HAVE BEEN COMING TO THE HUDSON Valley for the past 40 years and have developed a deep love for its natural beauty and landscape. When we began to plan for a retirement home, we knew this was where we wanted to be. As an architect, I had always dreamed of designing my own home, and when we found this piece of land with a view not only of the Catskill Mountains but also the Hudson River, we were ecstatic. Not surprisingly, there was a reason why what seemed to be a prime piece of property had yet to be developed. Site restrictions had effectively prevented previous owners from realizing the larger homes they had hoped to build on this former Christmas-tree farm, which had become overwhelmed with spruce.

A SITE-DRIVEN DESIGN

The lot is small and narrow—just 1.1 acres and a little more than 100 ft. at its widest. A third of the property is steeply sloped and unbuildable. A previous owner had commissioned extensive engineering plans, and the result was that the local board of health would only approve one building location and limited the size of the septic system to a two-bedroom dwelling. I was confident that I could work with the site restrictions, and with our children grown and out of the house, my wife and I were ready and willing to downsize our own living requirements.

The initial challenge was making the lot buildable. The site needed to be cleared, and the septic-system requirements called for 4 ft. of fill at the front of what would become our view. From the outset, we knew that the land-development costs would account for 25% of our budget. Understanding that before starting work on the design saved us a good deal of time, effort, and, ultimately, money. We carefully modeled details of the design and studied them closely, which allowed us to know almost exactly what the spaces would look and feel like before construction even began. As a result of that effort, we were better able to negotiate the site limitations and come up with a design that would suit our needs.

The plan came together quickly. Our starting point was the view. In order to take full advantage of the river and the mountains beyond, we wanted to have glass along the house's entire west-facing side. The result is generous amounts of light streaming in from the windows and doors at the first floor. A second row of windows adds even more natural light. The porch posts align with the structure of the window bays, minimizing obstructions to the light and view and helping to bring the outside in.

ON VIEW

Overgrown spruce from this
former tree farm obscured the site's
potential for majestic views. At 1.1 acres
and 100 ft. at its widest, the site came
with some burdensome restrictions on
allowable septic-system size and proximity to
neighbors. Careful planning and excavation allowed
the architect to push as close to the view as possible.

SEPTIC SYSTEM

VIEW

THE VALUE OF SITE-SPECIFIC DESIGN.
Working within strict site parameters,
architect Philip Ivory demonstrated
an exceptional unity of design and
aesthetics in service of a single goal:
to maximize and integrate the view to
make this small home live large.

However, the sunlight can be overwhelming at times, so we installed remotely operated roll shades from Hunter Douglas. Heat gain has proved not to be an issue. Open windows on the first and second floors coupled with ceiling fans provide a cooling flow of air when needed, and generously sized gable vents support a positive draft up to and through the attic space.

The extensive use of windows and doors in this two-story design required a rigid structure to counteract potential lateral loads. This could not be accomplished by means of wood framing unless we were to sacrifice window area for framed-wall area. My engineer and I settled on a steel-frame structure that forms three bays around the windows and doors, with a major beam above extending the entire length of the west wall. The columns and beam were sized to be concealed within the 2x6 frame wall, with web stiffeners introduced at the connections. Ultimately, the steel frame represented maximum strength while requiring the minimum amount of wall area.

OPEN PLAN

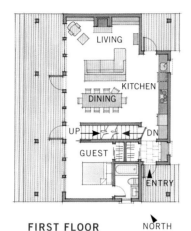

FIRST FLOOR   NORTH   SECOND FLOOR   0 2 4   8 FT.

SPECS
Bedrooms: 2
Bathrooms: 2
Size: 1,280 sq. ft.
Cost: $225 per sq. ft.
Completed: 2014
Location: Hudson, N.Y.
Architect: Philip Ivory Architects,
ivorymchugh.com
Builder: J.R. Romanchuk and Sons,
romanchukandsons.com

MAKING A SMALL HOUSE LIVE LARGE

In my residential practice in Philadelphia, kitchens and bathrooms commonly receive a significant amount of attention. That was not the case with this design, where the kitchen and the bathrooms are modest and the details of the open living space received more energy. A lot of consideration went into the look and size of the windows and the doors—how they space out along the length of the wall, where the meeting rails fall in relationship to eye level, and so on. I played with the scale of the openings. The double-hung windows on the west wall are oversize, matching the 8-ft.-tall doors and accentuating the verticality of the space. The horizontal line of the meeting rails is a counterpoint to the vertical and permits an unobstructed view whether one is seated or standing. The net result is that the space feels much larger than it actually is.

Furniture establishes the spaces in our open plan, so those choices were critical. We started with items we knew we wanted and then designed a few custom pieces. For example, the sectional sofa defines the space in front of, and circulation around, the woodstove. The widths and lengths of the furniture had to be considered to ensure adequate circulation around everything. We had a custom sideboard built to match the length of the sofa, which also establishes the edge of the dining area. Its height matches the dimensions of the sofa, and it's deep enough to provide useful storage without encroaching on the space around the dining table. At a dinner party with 10 people, there is plenty of space to circulate freely.

Sharing space is another strategy to make this small house live large. Except for the bathrooms and closets, a pocket door to the guest room is the only interior door separating public and private living areas.

The master bedroom is on the second floor. All furniture is concealed behind walls, creating privacy but never entirely cutting those spaces off from the public areas. The second-floor balcony allows for direct communication down to the living, dining, and kitchen areas.

The walls and trim are painted a soft white. The windows and doors are whitewashed to accentuate the wood grain and to prevent the natural yellowing of unstained pine. These subtle finishes reflect the natural light, contribute to the expansive feel of the space, and frame the most significant colors—those from the landscape.

MAKING A VISION A VIEW

We were regular visitors to the site at every stage of construction and even camped out inside the shell once the roof was on. This is not a practice

A GAME OF SCALE

1 A mass of built-in bookcases shifts your attention to the windows and view when first entering the room but creates a sense of intimacy when you're sitting by the fireplace.

2 The view through the 8-ft.-tall doors and full-height windows is optimized by keeping the sightlines free of any obstructions. For the exterior, that meant aligning the porch posts to the window frames. For the interior, there is no furniture taller than the dining chairs, which subtly adds to a sense of the space's volume.

3 The furniture was planned carefully around selected pieces and then supplemented with custom infill pieces to allow the maximum use of space without sacrificing a comfortable flow of traffic.

I would recommend to my clients, but for my wife and me, it was a wonderful way to feel more engaged in this personal process. Our builder was very accommodating.

On every project, I believe that a team needs to be built among the architect, the client, and the builder. Experience has taught me that this team formation and good communication are critical to a project's success. Having someone listen to exactly what we were trying to accomplish was essential. That sounds obvious, but it rarely works out that way. It's not always easy on contractors when architects work on their own homes, but we developed a great working relationship with Jim Romanchuk and his crew. And they told us they were happy because as they worked, they got to enjoy the view.

WALL OF LIGHT. A frameless pocket door with a recessed track runs from floor to ceiling. Used to close off the guest bedroom when there is a need for privacy, it's usually left open to keep the natural light flowing into the house along the western wall.

ABOVE LEFT AND RIGHT: PUSH AND PULL. To create second-floor living space under the steep roof, the architect designed a shed dormer for the front of the house. In the back, however, he recessed the roof to allow a better view from the second-floor balcony.

ABOVE THE TIDE

Storm-resistant building regulations inspired this home's architects to give it a better view of its beautiful coastal site

BY KILEY JACQUES

THE MAIN CHALLENGE POSED BY THIS SITE HAD to do with its proximity to Long Island Sound. Recently amended FEMA regulations specify new builds be 13 ft. above mean tide. Because the grade here is at 6 ft., Fairfax & Sammons had to raise the finished floor by 7 ft. The difficulty was trying to make a Cape-style house—which would normally sit right on the ground—look natural when elevated. The treatment of the exposed foundation wall was paramount. They took advantage of the required mounded septic system by bringing it up to one corner of the house and surrounding it with retaining walls. This provided visual continuity to the exposed foundation wall, which was faced with handmade brick in Flemish bond. Openings to let the storm surge flow under the house were mandated and located below the windows to emphasize the vertical line of the fenestration. The height of the house allowed for a platform deck on the rear with views across the water. The elevation also disguises a raised pool.

Designer: Fairfax & Sammons
Builder: Morton Buildings, mortonbuildings.com;
         Coastline Building Contractors
Location: West Neck, N.Y.
Photos: Durston Saylor, durstonsaylor.com

SMALL HOUSE HAS IT ALL

A little house
on an urban
infill lot leaves
room for
gardens and
play, and lives
larger than
its diminutive
footprint

BY DUNCAN
MCPHERSON

WHEN NEW CLIENTS DAVE AND ALI APPROACHED us to design a tiny house on an awkward, urban infill lot, we were excited by the challenge, but skeptical that the project would make it past the conceptual stage. They had a tight budget and a 0.2-acre parcel, which sloped steeply away from the street, and wanted to build a 500-sq.-ft. house, leaving some land for a miniature farm. After meeting Dave and Ali, we could tell they were serious and wanted professional help to create an efficient floor plan and make the most of their tricky lot.

They wanted the home to reflect their values of a simple life with less stuff, but realized the need to balance these things against the practicalities of modern living. laundry machines, computers, a TV, and amenities for entertaining friends. Their home life centered on cooking great meals, gardening, and raising chickens, and a fully functional kitchen was a must-have. Their larger design goals included lots of outdoor living space and daylight, as well as privacy.

The house's placement on the lot was critical to meeting these goals. The land is in an up-and-coming neighborhood, one block away from shops and restaurants, and came with its own set of challenges: car traffic, a steep dropoff from the road, a small buildable area, and a perennial creek at the rear. We quickly realized that the parking needed to stay tight to the street to minimize the cost of a driveway and to conserve land for other uses. Siting the house on the low portion of the lot partially screens it from the street, and creates intimate spaces for the screened porch and yard. A simple shed roof that opens up toward the road makes room for windows that bring in natural light from that side of the house. The living spaces and porch are oriented toward the private and wooded back portion of the land. With its ceiling following the plane of the roof, wall of windows, and white interior, the living space feels large and light. Terracing the gardens into the slope saved the remaining flat areas for outdoor living.

Creating functional back-of-house space was another design challenge. We settled on dedicating one room to multiple functions: laundry, bathroom, mudroom, storage, and back entry. Packing these together meant reconsidering the traditional compartments of a home. Maximizing wall space for storage and combining the floor area of spaces for circulation meant designing and considering every last inch of space. After careful assembly of this design puzzle, all of these separate functions interconnect in the space comfortably.

LITTLE HOUSE ON A TRICKY LOT. Samsel Architects' very small house makes sensible use of a difficult lot, providing the owners with the simplicity and outdoor space they wanted, an interior that lives larger than its footprint, and almost unimaginable levels of privacy for a tiny, urban lot.

EVERYTHING IN 816 SQ. FT.

The owners wanted a highly functional kitchen and a strong connection between indoor and outdoor spaces. The bathroom, laundry, and mudroom would often get their own dedicated spaces in a larger home but were combined here to maximize the use of the available square footage.

FIRST FLOOR

KITCHEN

BEDROOM

DINING

SCREENED PORCH

ENTRY

LOFT LADDER

BATHROOM/LAUNDRY/ UTILITY/MUDROOM

NORTH ►

SECOND FLOOR

OPEN TO BELOW

LOFT

DN

0 2 4   8 ft.

SPECS

Bedrooms: 1

Bathrooms: 1

Size: 816 sq. ft.

Cost: $204 per sq. ft.

Completed: 2015

Location: Asheville, N.C.

Architect: Samsel Architects, samselarchitects.com

Builder: Beach Hensley Homes

There was one hiccup—and it's a lesson for anyone who wants a tiny home: the lender was loath to back a 500-sq.-ft. house. To secure financing, Dave and Ali had to upsize their plans. We were able to adjust the roofline and massing of the house to add 300 sq. ft., including a habitable loft of more than 200 sq. ft., without adding much to the construction costs. The loft, accessed by a ladder, became critical for the house to meet Dave and Ali's needs when their family suddenly grew by one. The baby took over the bedroom, and Dave and Ali moved their bed into the loft.

The construction budget was such that every stick of wood was considered. One problem inherent in small homes is the economy of scale; the cost per square foot for small homes is typically higher than for larger homes. We worked with the builder during the design phase to talk through the best assemblies and most cost-effective material options. We settled on a conventional framing

BORROWERS BEWARE

Wanting a simple life with less stuff, the owners had their hearts set on a 500-sq.-ft. home. This goal was upended by the realities of the lending industry, and provides a lesson for anyone who wants a tiny home. Lenders typically rely on the values of comparable homes nearby—known as "comparables" or "comps"—when making loan decisions, and there was nothing in the neighborhood that was similar to what the owners wanted. To secure financing, the owners had to upsize their plans.

Adjusting the footprint and bumping up the roof of the house allowed for the inclusion of a more than 200-sq.-ft. habitable loft and increased the overall size by about 300 sq. ft. without adding much to the construction costs. A ladder off the dining area accesses the loft, as a full stair would have taken up too much floor area.

system on a crawlspace foundation, which provided tight but much-needed storage space. We minimized constructed corners and maximized connectivity from inside spaces to the screened porch. This inside-outside connection allows the house to live larger for at least three seasons of the year.

Energy efficiency was also a priority, and spray-foam insulation was used to create a tight building envelope. The small-house design is perfect for a minisplit heating and cooling system with two wall units, one in the living area and one in the bedroom. A ceiling fan in the living area and an exhaust fan in the bathroom help circulate the conditioned air throughout the house. Simple interior finishes and IKEA cabinets helped keep costs down, while fiber-cement siding and a metal roof bring durability to the exterior.

EIGHT DESIGN LESSONS FROM A SMALL HOUSE ON A SLOPED LOT

1 URBAN PRIVACY
Located about a block from a popular street packed with restaurants and shopping, the 0.2-acre lot has plenty of close neighbors and road traffic. Beginning on a small, flat spot next to the road, the property slopes steeply before flattening out again and backing into a treeline along a stream. The slope provided some challenges for construction, but locating the house at the bottom of the hill means the contours of the land provide a natural privacy buffer for the yard and home. With the slope screening the house from the street, the wall of windows in the dining area floods the space with natural light without compromising privacy. Locating the living space and screen porch at the back of the home accentuates the sense of solitude.

2 COMBINED SPACE
Designing areas to serve multiple functions helps maximize the space of a small home. The bathroom, laundry, and utilities, as well as a second entrance with a mudroom, are combined into a roughly 80-sq.-ft. space in the back of the house (technically the front), leaving more room for the living area where the occupants spend most of their time.

3 LIGHT AND SIZE
To get light into the home from the street side, a shed roof slopes up toward the street and extends vertically above it, and the space below the roof—on three sides of the loft—is filled with windows. The sloped ceiling, which follows the line of the shed roof down to the living area, combined with the white interior and natural light from all of the windows, makes the inside space feel larger. The sense of space is further extended by a window wall in the dining area that visually connects the space to the garden and yard, and a large sliding glass door that connects the living area to the 200-sq.-ft. screened porch allows the home to live a little bit larger for three seasons of the year.

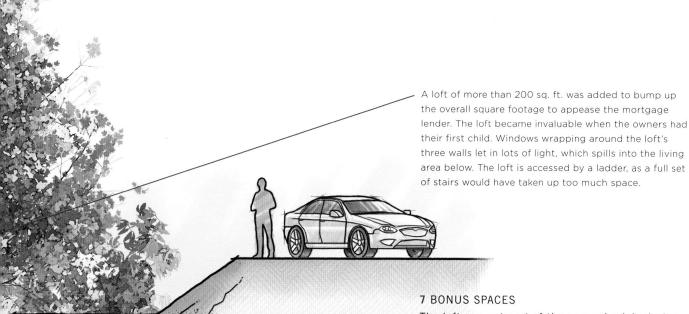

A loft of more than 200 sq. ft. was added to bump up the overall square footage to appease the mortgage lender. The loft became invaluable when the owners had their first child. Windows wrapping around the loft's three walls let in lots of light, which spills into the living area below. The loft is accessed by a ladder, as a full set of stairs would have taken up too much space.

4 ECONOMY OF SCALE

There's often an advantage to buying in bulk; the unit cost tends to decrease as you buy more. The same is generally true of homes—as the square footage increases, the cost per square foot goes down. There's no economy of scale when you build small, but one way to pare the cost per square foot is to build up rather than out, since site work and foundations generally cost more per square foot than framing lumber and sheet goods. Bumping up the roof to make room for a habitable loft of more than 200 sq. ft. added little extra cost to this home.

5 STORAGE SOLUTIONS

The bedroom has two closets for clothes and a hatch to access the crawlspace, which holds seasonally used items. IKEA cabinetry wraps around two walls of the kitchen, which also has a small island with shelf space. Shelves and a closet in the multifunctional bathroom/laundry room/mudroom provide additional capacity. The owners also designed a dining bench that has storage inside.

6 DURABLE MATERIALS

Fiber-cement siding and a metal roof contribute to the home's simple, modern aesthetic, as well as the overall durability of the exterior. Both can endure years of weather and sun with minimal maintenance.

7 BONUS SPACES

The loft was not part of the owners' original plan, and it was used very infrequently when they first moved in. They spent much of their time on the screened porch, a 200-sq.-ft. space that allows the home to live significantly larger for at least three seasons of the year. Once the owners had a baby, though, the loft became critical for the home to continue to work for the family. The baby took over the bedroom, and the owners moved their bed to the loft.

8 SLOPE SOLUTIONS

Terracing gardens into the existing slope and locating parking above the house and adjacent to the street helps to maximize the usability and privacy of the lot's rear flat area for play. A second entryway, facing the street, opens into a combined bathroom, laundry, and mudroom—a solution that left more space for the living area and bedroom.

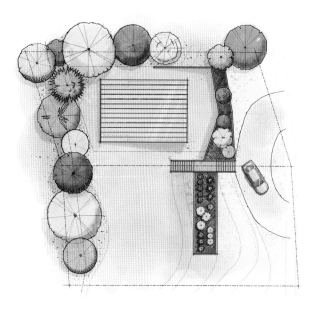

LIVING LARGER. The screened porch connects
to the living area, allowing the home to expand
in the warmer seasons. The porch and views
through it give the house a strong connection
to the outside space, and the porch's location
at the back of the home provides privacy.

LEFT LIGHT AND PRIVACY. Locating the house at the bottom of the lot's steep slope provides a natural privacy buffer, allowing for lots of natural light without compromising privacy.

BELOW KITCHEN ESSENTIAL. A highly functional kitchen was a must-have for the owners, who do most of their own cooking and like to entertain. The ceiling follows the line of the shed roof, making the living space feel large and airy while providing plenty of wall space for windows to brighten the home and enhance its connection to the outdoors.

Part 2

CABINS AND UNIQUE RETREATS

SHINGLE-STYLE REMODEL

A cramped single-story cabin grows up

BY MATTHEW SWETT

THIS PROJECT BEGAN WITH A BIRTHDAY PRESENT. Kathy, who attends my wife's yoga classes, learned that I'm an architect, and asked if she could gift some of my time to her husband, David, to help him design a small woodshop. Kathy, I soon discovered, is an avid weaver. She didn't know it at the time, but I had grown up in a woodshop making weaving looms with my parents. We were well matched.

A few hours consultation evolved into a full design for the woodshop. We worked well together and our collective attention turned next to their house. Kathy and David were nearing retirement and were considering transitioning from their home in Seattle to their property here on Whidbey Island. The existing cabin was a mere 800 sq. ft., and downsizing from their four-story Craftsman-style home was too much of a leap for the couple. However, they realized they could make it work with some thoughtful modifications.

THE SITE STEERS DESIGN

The cabin was old—the first of its kind built at Bush Point. As such, it was well sited, high on the hill with sweeping views of the Salish Sea. Age added grace—over the years, the landscape had grown and the house had been enfolded in a mature grove of trees.

The building itself was small and oddly laid out. It lacked an entry; you arrived via French doors directly into the kitchen. The bathroom and bedrooms were tight and, in our rainy climate, the large, uncovered front deck was seldom used. The mechanical system was an afterthought, tacked on to the side of the building some time in the last century. It needed some help.

Early in the design process, we agreed that stewarding the landscape was a high priority, so we decided to keep the footprint as close to the original as possible. We tried to retain as much of the existing structure as we could but soon learned that was impractical. The existing ceilings were too low, the framing insubstantial, and the energy performance poor. The one bonus was that the foundation system had been upgraded in the recent past. Constrained on all sides, but with a solid foundation under us, we decided to marginally increase the footprint and add a second floor above. Ultimately, that meant nearly starting over on the existing foundation. Kathy and David had spent a considerable amount of time refurbishing the cabin's interior woodwork already (see the sidebar p. 112), so in the interest of preserving that resource and history, they carefully removed it for reinstallation in the new structure.

CREATING A CLASSIC LOOK. The cabin original to the site was cramped and squat, and its uncovered outdoor living space went unused much of the time. The remodeled house is everything the old structure was not. Designed in the farmhouse style, it has a covered porch, soaring gables, and an all-wood exterior that glows with inviting warmth. The wood's natural finish is complemented by the dark tones of the windows and roof, giving the exterior a simple yet striking appearance. The windows have traditional divided lites, but in most cases they're limited to the top sash for uninterrupted views.

A FLOORPLAN WITH FLEXIBILITY

The bedrooms are on the darker northern side of the house to encourage sound sleep. The primary living areas are on the south side, making the spaces brighter and providing water views. There are living rooms, full bathrooms, and bedrooms on both floors, giving both the owners and guests privacy and allowing the owners to live on one level as they age.

SPECS
Bedrooms: 2
Bathrooms: 2
Size: 2,100 sq. ft.
Location: Whidbey Island, Wash.
Architect: Matthew Swett, Taproot Architects, Langley, Wash., taproot.us
Builder: Sound Construction LLC, soundconstructionsw.com

1 Kitchen
2 Dining
3 Parlor
4 Landing
5 Bedroom
6 Weaving studio/ future bedroom

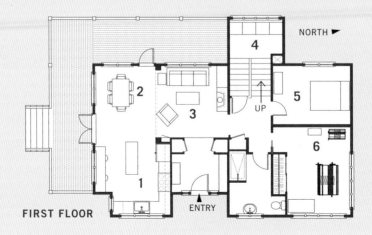

NORTH ▶

0 2 4   8 ft.

FIRST FLOOR

ENTRY

PLAN FOR AGING IN PLACE. The weaving room can be closed off from the rest of the first-floor living space by closing a reclaimed five-panel door. The room can become a first-floor master bedroom should the owners decide they no longer want to use the stairs.

MODERN KITCHEN WITH A PERIOD LOOK. The kitchen's period-look fir cabinets were built by a local craftsman using reclaimed straight-grain fir. Soapstone countertops, period-style lighting, and a large apron-front sink complement the home's farmhouse style.

A HARDWORKING, COMPACT PLAN

It was a bit of a challenge to fit everything my clients wanted into the available area, but a few key decisions made it work. We split the living area across the floors. This resulted in a modest parlor on the lower floor and a more generous living room on the second floor, where there is better access to the views. This allowed us to closely follow the original house plan, with the bedrooms on the north side and the living areas on the south.

A small addition for the stairs provided just enough room for a walk-out laundry room on the first landing and a built-in window seat on the landing above.

We added a wraparound porch on the view side of the house. Aesthetically, this helped to shape the home into its farmhouse character. Functionally, the porch extends the living space outward, providing shelter in inclement weather and even transforming into a kennel for Loki and Sunna, the family dogs.

SALVAGED-STOCK INTERIOR

The original cabin's floors and walls were covered almost entirely with Douglas fir. We spent several months removing as much of the wood as we could with Burke bars and a host of pry bars. The boards were then resawn to create wainscoting, ceiling boards, and the coat rack and bench near the entrance. Some of the boards became walls in our workshop. The interior doors came from Ballard Reuse in Seattle. One side of the doors was varnished and the other heavily painted.

We used a low-temperature heat gun to remove the paint from the flat surfaces and 3M Safest Stripper on molded sections. After applying the stripper, we left it covered with plastic for 4 to 6 hours and then removed the softened paint with coarse steel wool and an assortment of scraping tools. After removing the paint, we sanded the surface to 120 grit with a Bosch

random-orbit sander. Smaller areas were sanded with a small belt sander and a Fein oscillating multitool. The smallest areas were sanded by hand. After the doors were finished with two coats of water-based polyurethane, a local craftsman prepped them and hung them on jambs. Whenever possible, we used period or reproduction hinges and hardware.

—Kathy Stetz, the homeowner

Steel railings atop trolleys telescope out from behind fixed railings to close off the stairs. This provides an easy transition between human and canine needs. Last but not least, the structure of the porch discretely encloses 5,000 gal. of rainwater collection beneath it.

The scope of the renovation allowed us to address the issue of aging in place. The enlarged bathroom provides a wheelchair-friendly environment with a roll-in shower, and the weaving room can be utilized as a future master bedroom. These two features ensure that essential needs can be provided on the main floor. The few steps up from grade at the entry are a result of the existing foundation, but they can easily be addressed with a modest ramp if and when needed.

EFFICIENT SHELL, RECLAIMED DETAILS

Kathy and David's historic home in Seattle was chronically cold, so they wanted their new home to be more comfortable. We addressed that need with a quality building envelope and a multilayered heating system. The envelope contains R-28 double-stud walls filled with dense-pack cellulose, a high-R-value roof (R-59) and a better-than-code (R-38) floor system. Air leakage is a big part of envelope performance, so we taped the sheathing joints and used fluid-applied flashing around window and door openings.

To complement the envelope, we installed a heat-recovery ventilator to ensure the home has a steady supply of clean, fresh air. The ventilation system has high-performance filtration that helps keep

STAIR TOWER MAKES IT WORK

The second floor contains the master bedroom, a full bath, and a comfortable living area with a propane fireplace (photo above). Like the first-floor living room, the upstairs living area has south-facing water views. The stair tower, an 8-ft. by 10-ft. addition to the original footprint, connects the first and second floors and provides a refuge in the form of a reading nook on its oversize landing (see the top photo on p. 114).

SECOND FLOOR

1 Living area
2 Master suite
3 Closet
4 Landing
5 Storage
6 Mechanicals

RIGHT: MORE THAN A STAIRWAY. The staircase to the second floor has a window seat at the landing—a perfect spot for reading a book or enjoying a cup of coffee. Underneath the landing is an 8-ft. by 10-ft. laundry room with grade-level access to the outdoors.

BELOW: MODERN BATH WITH TIME-LESS APPEAL. The 10-ft. by 10-ft. upstairs bath has 1-in. hexagonal floor tile, period fixtures, and white subway tile that give the bath a historic look with modern conveniences. The toilet is tucked into an alcove adjacent to the shower.

MAKING ROOM FOR INSULATION

The house has staggered double-stud walls filled with dense-pack cellulose insulation. The roof is also superinsulated with stacked pairs of rafters arranged like a truss with top and bottom chords. The deep space provides more room for cellulose insulation above the sloping ceiling, and the space between the rafter pairs acts as a thermal break. The unusual rafter arrangement has a second benefit: The upper rafter creates the exposed rafter tail with the right proportions to complement the rest of the exterior.

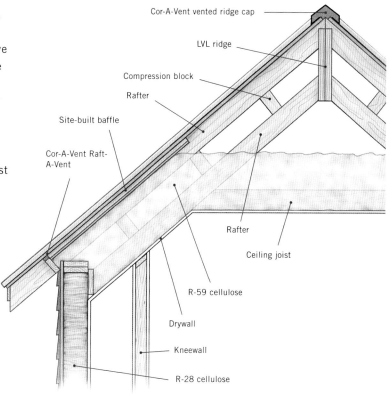

Cor-A-Vent vented ridge cap
LVL ridge
Compression block
Rafter
Site-built baffle
Cor-A-Vent Raft-A-Vent
Rafter
Ceiling joist
R-59 cellulose
Drywall
Kneewall
R-28 cellulose

pet fur and dander under control. The heating system consists of traditional floor-mounted radiators heated by an electric boiler coupled with radiant-tile heat mats and propane fireplaces to ensure that the home will stay warm, even in a power outage.

Climate change and seismic activity in our area continue to encourage us to think about how best to support personal and community needs in the event of disrupted services. In addition to the enhanced thermal envelope, this home also has a backup generator, heating system, and water storage on hand. The thinking is simple: If our needs are met, we are more available to help others in need.

My clients wanted a home that expressed their attention to craft and appreciation of materials.

Much of the native fir used in the home was salvaged and resawn by a mill in nearby Port Townsend. The kitchen cabinets were hand-built in David's shop. Finish-carpentry details blend seamlessly into the architecture. My clients weren't spectators in this regard—Kathy spent countless hours restoring historic doors for use in the interior, while David used his woodworking skills to build the custom entry coat rack.

Overall, the house has a warm glow. It can be seen in the rich character of the interior and exterior woodwork, but it runs deeper. It's a feeling evoked when you walk through the space—it feels like home.

TWO CABINS INTO ONE

How a home with roots in early American history was transformed into a modern mountain retreat

BY ROB YAGID

NESTLED INTO THE WESTERN SLOPE OF JOBBER'S Mountain in northern Virginia sits the Hazel River Cabin, a home designed by Washington, D.C., architect David Haresign. While not everyone will find themselves in the position of redesigning a 226-year-old toll keeper's cabin to seamlessly connect with a 165-year-old addition and a relocated 181-year-old chestnut cabin to make a new home, Haresign's approach highlights lessons that are valuable to anyone remodeling an older home to accommodate a contemporary way of living while acknowledging and respecting its original character.

THE PROGRAM REVEALS ITSELF

When he purchased the property, Haresign's client, Joe, initially thought that he would have to tear down two poorly framed buildings. But after beginning demolition on the first structure, Joe discovered a 1795 toll keeper's log cabin beneath a layer of wood clapboards. He did some research and learned about the history of the site, the cabin, and its 1856 addition. Instead of proceeding with the tear-down, Joe hired a local log-cabin restoration contractor to make a more comprehensive assessment of the building and its potential.

With its small rooms and low, 7-ft.-6-in.-tall ceilings, the cabin would be much too cramped for the home that Joe envisioned. The contractor told Joe about an additional derelict cabin, the former chestnut slave quarters from Mountjoy Farm in Howard County, Maryland, that he could procure and bring to the site. Soon after, Haresign was brought on to marry the two.

Joe wanted to use the new home as a retreat. He wanted the design to create a memorable renovation that would respect the existing character of the cabins; celebrate the beauty of the logs, wood framing, and stone fireplaces; and incorporate all of the conveniences of a modern home. The spatial program was simple: The new home would need a large modern kitchen that opened into the main living area and a dining room that could comfortably accommodate six to eight people. Joe wanted a library that could also double as an additional sleeping space. The home would need to accommodate two bedrooms, each with a private bath, with a sitting area or study nearby. These amenities, as well as an equipment room for modern mechanicals, would all need to be confined within a 2,500-sq.-ft. home.

The original toll keeper's cabin

The chestnut cabin

LINKING LOGS

David Haresign of Bonstra Haresign Architects was charged with combining two historic structures into a singular design. When viewed from the west, the original 226-year-old toll keeper's cabin sits to the left of its 1856, white-clapboard-covered addition. A former chestnut slave quarters salvaged from Mountjoy Farm in Maryland has its gable facing west and is joined to the 1856 structure with a narrow modern addition made mostly of glass.

MODERN VIEWS. The living room looks out to a view of Old Rag Mountain through semicustom Andersen Eagle windows. Most of the units in the home replicate windows of historical proportions. These units were arranged as a reinterpretation of divided-lite windows to add a bit of whimsy and complexity. A modern Wittus woodstove stands in the corner with minimal connection to the old cabin.

CONTEXTUAL MODERNISM

Some may have looked at these cabins and set out to restore them instead of transforming them into something new and different. But today, we use spaces very differently than when these cabins were originally constructed. For restorations, renovations, additions, and adaptive-use projects, Haresign employs a simple design principle that he calls "contextual modernism." He aims to add new elements, like modern technology and precisely manufactured components that respect and celebrate the character of the original structure, yet remain clearly contemporary.

For example, in this home, the newer elements are not hidden or blended into the old structure in any way. The modern additions, like the steel support beams, stand in stark contrast to the original structure. And while steel is a more modern material—clearly from a different period than the original log structure—it also expresses an essential, rough-hewn character that lets the two materials work remarkably well together.

While new, modern materials were utilized throughout the remodel, the team prioritized reusing the original logs whenever possible. There were several species in the original buildings, as cabin

MATERIALS IN THEIR NATIVE STATE. Steel I-beams under
the bedroom allowed for as much clear space over the
kitchen as possible. The fabricated steel has a rawness that
complements the hewn logs. The steel railing, which mirrors
the chinking in the walls, is a reinterpretation of local cattle
gates. Cherry is used for stair treads and post inserts.

LOGIC IN THE LAYOUT

The kitchen and main first-floor living space were positioned in the chestnut cabin, beneath a lofted master bedroom. A second bedroom, full bathroom, and mechanical room sit within the basement below the living area. The dining room is set in the 1856 addition and shares a double-sided fireplace with a den in the old 1794 toll keeper's cabin. A lofted library and study area, which doubles as additional sleeping quarters, overlooks the space.

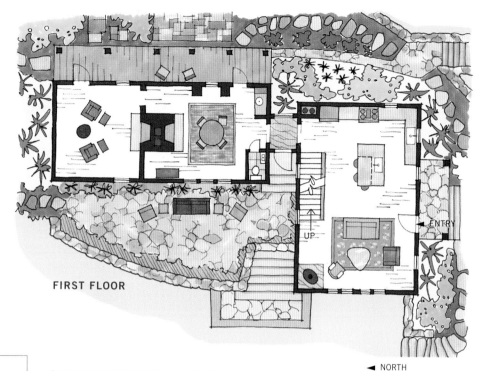

FIRST FLOOR

◀ NORTH

SPECS
Bedrooms: 2
Bathrooms: 2½
Size: 2,400 sq. ft.
Design: David Haresign, Bonstra Haresign Architects, bonstra.com
Builder: Greg Foster, Timberbuilt Construction, timberbuiltconstruction.com

OPEN TO BELOW

DN

SECOND FLOOR

OPEN TO BELOW

0 2 4   8 FT.

builders used whatever was available at the time. Oak, chestnut, and pine were predominant, and had survived the test of time.

The team also sought to use reclaimed materials as much as possible, either from the existing cabins or from sources in the immediate vicinity. Eighty percent of the wood floors were reclaimed. While this home is not a technical restoration, Haresign clearly aimed to finish each cabin with a nod to its long history.

A COHESIVE DESIGN

All of the structures—the original log cabins, the 1856 frame addition, and the most current modern addition—have their own unique attributes. Instead of meddling with the elements in an effort to create a home with a universal feel from space-to-space, the design and build team embraced and showcased the contrasting elements. The differences in these spaces and materials, which can be severe in certain instances, helped create a clear composition. Walking through the home, an observer can easily understand the age of each space and its relationship to the present and to the past.

MAGIC MOUNTAIN CABIN

This elegant and functional cabin creates the illusion of spaciousness with thoughtful finishes and storage solutions

BY AARON FAGAN

AMONG THE TREES ON A WEST-FACING KNOLL overlooking Vermont's Mad River Valley sits this compact cabin. Architect Joan Heaton says that *low maintenance, energy efficient, modern,* and *edgy* are among the terms the homeowner used to describe her initial vision for this one-level cabin. The finished home embodies those words in a variety of ways.

Polished concrete floors with radiant heat and a modern woodstove keep the cabin warm and stylish. The look of the floors combines nicely with the clean lines of the tongue-and-groove ceiling and the sleek built-ins. The cabinet wall and eating nook in the kitchen demonstrate how adequate storage allows a small home to function efficiently. European appliances and contemporary fixtures contribute to the kitchen's proportion, modernity, and spaciousness.

Transoms and bifold doors at the southwest corner of the cabin create open views, and the doors provide access to a deck that increases living space. One of the things that Heaton likes best about designing small houses is that they offer an opportunity to use windows on all sides to draw in daylight, provide multiple views, and allow for cross ventilation. In concert with an open plan, limited interior partitions, and connection to the outdoors, such windows make small houses feel much bigger than they actually are.

The exterior has durable, stained cedar siding, clad windows, and a standing-seam metal roof. A separate one-car garage with PV panels and a charging station for an electric car rounds out this home's goals for efficiency and sustainability.

The homeowner chose to use large slabs of stone on the walls in the master and guest baths. With no grout lines, they create a visually rich and uninterrupted field, particularly in the barrier-free shower and tub area of the master bath, where simple design elements create a feeling of serenity and openness.

BICYCLE DECK. At the southwest corner of the cabin, bifold doors open to views and seamless access to a deck that increases living space and that provides room for outdoor bicycle training.

TRICK OF THE EYE

Allowing the living room to spill out onto the deck adds livable space and a connection to the outdoors. An alcove with a closet provides necessary storage and a clever buffer between the living area and the bedrooms. A bump-out for the tub adds a feature to the master bath and visual interest to the exterior.

SPECS
Bedrooms: 2
Bathrooms: 2
Size: 925 sq. ft.
Completed: 2015
Location: Waitsfield, Vt.
Architect: Joan Heaton, joanheatonarchitects.com
Builder: Brothers Building Co., brothersbuilding.com

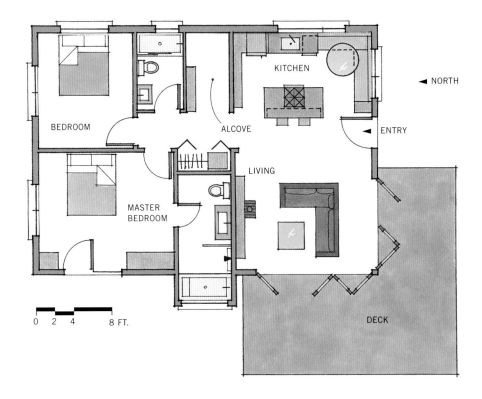

KITCHEN

NORTH

ALCOVE

ENTRY

BEDROOM

LIVING

MASTER
BEDROOM

0 2 4   8 FT.

DECK

According to Heaton, one of the biggest challenges of this project was accommodating the homeowner's hobbies—collecting wine, art, and bikes and training equipment for Iron Woman competitions. An early design included a dedicated training room, but in the final, smaller design, the wine and weights are in the guest bedroom, a bike is on a stationary trainer in the living room, and the art is rotated from a storage area in the alcove that also serves as a mudroom and a storage area for skis, bicycles, and other outdoor gear and apparel.

"Small homes are my favorite type of project because they include only essential spaces and have huge possibilities for relating to the site and surroundings," Heaton says. "My forward-thinking clients choose small homes because they value quality over quantity and also because such homes use fewer resources and consume less energy."

ABOVE AND RIGHT: THE SECRET OF STORAGE. Wall cabinets keep appliances organized and out of view, while an eating nook with various built-in drawers shows how storage can be used to make a small home function efficiently.

ALL THE RIGHT ANGLES. The barrier-free shower and tub area of the master bath is surrounded with stone slabs that combine with the concrete floor, floating vanity, glass partition, and window to create a sense of peaceful spaciousness.

NO DREARY DAYS

This well-crafted island home combines abundant windows with inviting nooks to create a subtle and sophisticated design

BY BRIAN PONTOLILO

SUSAN STOLTZ AND DAVID KAU'S CLIENTS, CARY and Linda Moore, had a simple request: They wanted "no dreary days" in their new home. But this is Orcas Island, off the Washington coast, where over 28 in. of rain falls annually, where summers can be cool and foggy, and where winter temps dip into the 30s.

Cary and Linda had some other requirements for the project, too. One spoke to their history (a *hikie'e,* a type of traditional Hawaiian daybed), another to the spectacular site (the house sits lightly on the land), and another to their lifestyle (the kitchen's cooking arrangement is quite unique). But to achieve "no dreary days," Susan and David had to make the home's open spaces luminous and the views abundant when the sun is shining. And when the sky turns cold and gray, they had to provide comfort, charm, and character to warm the soul. Susan and David achieved "no dreary days" and much more on this project. Their brilliance is apparent even before you enter the front door.

The approach to the house is a natural stone path that meanders through a landscape of rocks, native shrubs, and moss. At a glance, the prevailing single-story gable on the public-facing elevation imparts a modest feel. Sitting softly beneath a towering fir tree, the house is clad in fibercement and corrugated-metal siding and has a metal roof. These materials were chosen for their ability to withstand the harsh island environment. The clean lines and subtle exterior trim suggest simplicity, although a closer look at the house reveals a much more sophisticated design.

A bump-out around the western corner of the front-facing facade hints at a recurring theme of the plan: inviting nooks for various activities. All around the foundation, cantilevers come into view, a measure taken to disturb as little of the landscape as possible. For the same reason, all excavation was done from within the home's footprint.

With the cantilevers, corner windows on both sides of the house and on the bump-out conspire to create the illusion that the house is floating above the slender ridge on which it dwells. Eventually, it becomes clear that the east wing of the house is not square to the gable end. It is set at an obtuse angle to preserve a fir tree behind the home and to position the master suite for the best views. Even more subtle is the use of a shed roof over this wing rather than another gable. This allows the home to maintain a low profile to the public while rising toward the expanse of ocean, islands, and mountain peaks beyond.

Finally, at the entry, where an angled column and single beam support the roof and mark one's arrival, a view clear through the house to the landscape beyond is provided by a glass entry door.

NOOKS AND VIEWS. Perched on a precipice 1,200 ft. above sea level, this unassuming island home combines abundant windows for light and views with inviting nooks for cloudy-day refuge.

UNDER TOWERING FIR. This well-crafted new home on Orcas Island, Wash., designed by Stoltz Kau Architects, is equally suited to its natural surroundings and to its owners' distinctive sensibilities. At once, it is subtle and sophisticated.

HOME IS IN THE DETAILS

Cary and Linda call the house *Lanihuli,* which in Hawaiian means "swirling heavens," because the house is a great place to watch the island weather stir. And it's true: There are stunning views throughout this house. But the details inside are no less inspiring—from handsome trim elements to distinctive custom hardware to a variety of unique ceiling treatments. You don't have to go any farther than the entry to get the essence of what makes this home special.

Just inside the front door, Susan and David provide a preview of what's to come by pairing eye-level windows for views of the landscape with a set of windows placed high on the wall for views of the sky. A live-edge slab, milled from a Douglas-fir tree that was felled on-site, provides a place to sit and establishes another material theme—you'll find similar slabs in the master bedroom and in the kitchen. In fact, by the time you have seen the entire house, you'll have noticed six different local wood species used for flooring, cabinets, tables, counters, benches, and ceilings.

A COOKING KITCHEN

At a glance, this kitchen has all the essentials, but a closer look exposes an arrangement that is particular to how the homeowners cook. A pantry tucked behind the kitchen means less cabinetry in sight, leaving the sink wall free of uppers. Even the fridge is tucked slightly out of the way. Lit with plenty of daylight from two skylights, the island provides a worksurface and an entertaining and serving hub, and it distinguishes the kitchen from the great room.

Where a fridge or perhaps wall ovens might have been in a more conventional kitchen, there is a wood-fired pizza oven from EarthStone Ovens (earthstoneovens.com). A hearth and wood storage below hark back to the days when fireplace cooking was common. Though the kitchen island has a four-burner induction cooktop from Wolf (subzero-wolf.com), beneath the hood, the main cooking surface is a high-heat wok burner from Viking (vikingrange.com).

OPEN AND INTIMATE

Putting the home's private spaces just inside the entry allows the main living area, the great room in the back of the house, to have access to the best views. The den, home office, and public bathroom can double as a private guest suite. Snuck in behind the kitchen, the laundry area and a pantry allow the great room to be even more open and uncluttered.

SPECS

Bedrooms: 1
Bathrooms: 2
Size: 1,935 sq. ft.
Completed: 2012
Location: Orcas Island, Wash.
Architect: Stoltz Kau Architects, stoltzkau.com
Builder: White Construction & Co.

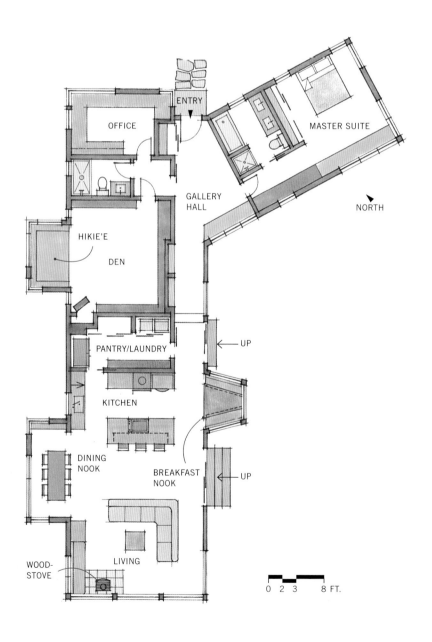

ENTRY

OFFICE

MASTER SUITE

GALLERY HALL

NORTH

HIKIE'E

DEN

UP

PANTRY/LAUNDRY

KITCHEN

DINING NOOK

BREAKFAST NOOK

UP

WOOD-STOVE

LIVING

0 2 3   8 FT.

DO NOT DISTURB. Though one goal of this project was to disturb as little of the landscape as possible, a small outdoor space was inevitable. The natural stone and organic shape of the patio blend well into the surroundings. Trellises overhang the windows to offer shade.

Susan and David describe Orcas Island as an architect's paradise, where first-rate builders and craftspeople thrive. It was because of one of these talented islanders, the local blacksmith, that the pair was able to incorporate one of the home's more elaborate details. Two rolling doors separate the entry from adjacent multipurpose spaces. Handmade by Jorgen Harle at Orcas Island Forge, the 37-ft.-long track and custom rollers are delightfully ingenious and functional.

From the entry, the home branches out in three directions. Through the rolling doors to the west are a den, a bath, and an office that can serve as a guest suite when needed. To the east is the master suite. Finally, a distinctive Douglas-fir ceiling detail—described by Susan as loosely inspired by Japanese architecture—draws you into a gallery hallway opening into a great room that includes the kitchen, dining nook, and living area.

A WARM WELCOME. The entry is celebrated with warm wood tones in the doors, cabinetry, and hallway ceilings. A live-edge bench hewn from Douglas fir reflects the natural surroundings and offers a place to sit. One-of-a-kind rolling-door hardware delights the craftsperson in all of us.

HAWAIIAN FOR "DAYBED." The bump-out bed in the den is inspired by the large, fixed couch known in Hawaiian as a *hikie'e*.

Critics of modern houses, with their large expanses of glass and open spaces, call the style cold and unwelcoming. Though the southern gable wall of this great room has nearly floor-to-ceiling windows that wrap both corners with views, the space is warm and comfortable. In fact, one of the most brilliant moves in this design is the placement of the woodstove. Sitting quietly in the corner of a panoramic aperture with an inboard inglenook at its side, it shifts the atmosphere from expansive to intimate.

There are two more intimate nooks around the great room—both for dining—and many more elements that create a sense of warmth and space. Perhaps most significant are the ceilings. The cathedral-style main ceiling is grounded by a pair

of hefty custom trusses and horizontal hemlock paneling that draw attention to the view on one end of the great room and the kitchen on the other. Both the breakfast nook and the main dining area are bump-outs whose lower ceilings help to distinguish them within the open space. Each has unique details that make it special, from the madrona tree-trunk pedestal and live-edge top of the breakfast table to the display shelves and corner window in the dining area.

Susan and David successfully established the themes of big views, quaint spaces, and special details in the entry and the great room, then carried them into the den and the master suite, where they continue to delight the homeowners and guests and to honor the island landscape.

DINNER IN THE FOREST. The large windows wrapping three sides of the breakfast nook (right) and dining bump-out (below) bring the surrounding scenery to the table.

A FRESH TAKE ON TRADITION

A renovation with a focus on increased space and sustainable systems transforms a historical home

BY DAVID T. HARESIGN

SITUATED ON A LARGE, GRASSY LOT IN THE WELL-established Washington, D.C., suburb of Chevy Chase, Md., this home was originally built in 1919 as a log cabin guesthouse handcrafted from Canadian cedar. While my design work is largely focused on mixed-use and multifamily infill buildings, I took on this whole-house renovation because of the home's unique history and the owner's passion for honoring it.

The client contacted me after seeing an article on the Hazel River Cabin project (see "Two Cabins Into One" on p. 116), which also respectfully transformed an old log cabin—plus two other historic structures—into a modern livable house. I relished an opportunity to work on a challenging, noteworthy residential project again, in a neighborhood I can most accurately describe as an incredible collection of eclectic houses.

The current owner, who grew up in the house, is only the third full-time resident. Her renovation goals involved making the house livable for just her family, while simultaneously creating a flexible entertaining space for the numerous fundraising events she hosts. She also asked us to prioritize sustainable features and energy-efficient systems. To accomplish these goals, the design team was tasked with turning a tangle of tiny, dark rooms into open, flowing spaces conducive to modern living that still preserve the structure's historical character. The desire to save existing old-growth trees on the property and the need to work within a tight budget also meant reusing an earlier addition commissioned by the client's mother.

SPACE INNOVATION

The existing floor plan's central cube was divided into a warren of rooms resulting in awkward circulation and obstructed sightlines. Accessing the addition meant climbing up and over the stair landing, for example. To balance the floor plan and create a strong central axis, we planned a two-story addition similar in form and placed directly opposite the original log great room. Our strategy was to improve the floor plan by transforming the central cube from a jumble of rooms into a single cohesive space serving as a physical and visual transition from the restored log great room to the new contemporary kitchen.

EVOLUTION IN SCALE. The cladding materials and dimensions of the addition are intended to respect the existing structure, with complementary choices such as cedar siding, standing-seam metal roofing, and divided lites in the large-scale windows.

HISTORY IN PERSPECTIVE. Restraint worked best in the story-and-a-half, 100-year-old log great room. Uplighting was added to emphasize volume of space, and openings were adjusted to provide a stronger sense of balance on the interior.

Removing walls leading to the older addition revealed an unpleasant surprise during construction: Work on this addition had compromised the structural integrity of the floor system. The addition involved cutting away big portions of the original exterior walls, and because the logs in log houses are used in tension, the second floor was about to fall into the first. This instability necessitated the demolition and rebuilding of the entire second floor. However, that created an opportunity to raise the height of the first-floor ceilings. Glass flooring adjacent to the stairwell brings natural light from a ridge skylight down into the basement. Directly across from those stairs sits a 10-ft.-long dining table repurposed from century-old logs.

Outside circulation also received a makeover. Exterior spaces were reorganized around the new footprint, strengthening ties to the generous yard on multiple levels. In the basement, dropping the floor and expanding it out beneath the new addition made space for an exercise room and guest suite. A wall of glass offers walk-out access to native landscaping on the west side. Above, a two-story box-bay window tower connects the open kitchen to an alfresco dining deck and floods the primary bedroom with southern light. Offset from the front door, a parking court overlaps with a proportionally square walkway leading to the entry steps and up to the full-width front patio.

NEW OLD HOUSE. The addition sits back from the facade and mimics the form of the great room on the opposite end. This thoughtful layout highlights the original forms and distinguishes new spaces as more modern living elements nested with the old.

MAKING AN ADDITION LOOK RIGHT

The three phases of this home's transformation are best understood using massing models, where the newest addition can be seen as the scaled reflection of an original east wing. The size of the addition not only accommodates the spatial demands of the homeowner, but it also helps provide visual balance to the entire structure and remedy problematic additions on the west-facing elevation. The addition in both size and detail is distinctly modern, as was the intention.

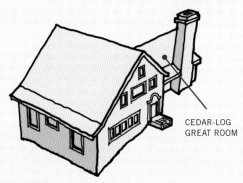

CEDAR-LOG GREAT ROOM

ORIGINAL 1919 CABIN

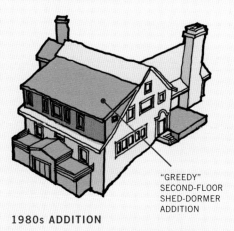

"GREEDY" SECOND-FLOOR SHED-DORMER ADDITION

1980s ADDITION

TWO-STORY ADDITION WITH NEW KITCHEN AND BEDROOM SUITE

2010s ADDITION

REBUILD AND RESTORE

Walls made from hand-split logs tend to be imprecise, so the entire house was out of square. Framing new walls within the log structure allowed for a tighter building envelope and rectilinear spaces. Our contractor's highly skilled framer—and a structural engineer specializing in historical buildings—deserves a ton of credit for restoring the structure of the house.

Despite the iconic look of an authentically constructed log cabin (the original owner brought Canadian lumberjacks down to assemble the giant cedars), the neighborhood elders instructed the current owner's mother to cover the exterior with stone for a more "luxury" facade when the addition was built in the 1980s.

Removing plaster and lath from interior walls revealed that most of the logs were damaged beyond restoration, and exposing them would also preclude making rooms more comfortable by insulating them, so the design team made the decision to insulate and cover them with drywall. The logs in the vaulted great room, however, remained nearly pristine. Our strategy here was to celebrate the history of the house by preserving the logs and original character of the great room. Logs were cleaned and new chinking inserted. Century-old casement windows were taken apart and then carefully restored or rebuilt as needed. A massive stone fireplace maintains the room's rustic atmosphere and provides visual and literal warmth for the voluminous space. Covering most other walls in crisp, white drywall, in contrast to the walls in the historical great room, generates a clear distinction between old and new.

Materials used in the new addition and renovated core relate to the log cabin while remaining decidedly modern. Natural-wood base cabinets, floating shelves, and the cooktop vent surround pay homage to the aged cedar finish in the great room. Historical casements were also restored in this space for continuity, while new oversize windows create a modern look. These old and new spaces are located on opposite ends of the house, with clear sightlines between them.

HISTORICAL INEFFICIENCIES

Not surprisingly, the old house was drafty in winter and hot in summer. Even with the added square footage of a new bedroom suite and kitchen, the owner uses a fraction of the power she did before—most of it renewable. New systems include electrical, plumbing, and high-efficiency, geothermal HVAC.

Superinsulation in the walls and ceilings—except in the great room—along with low-flow fixtures and energy-efficient appliances helped meet her environmental goals. A geothermal system keeps the open public areas comfortable year-round with little drain on the city grid. Original casement windows were painstakingly rebuilt with insulated floating glass, and exposed log walls in the story-and-a-half great room were repointed for a tighter building envelope. Outside, a permeable parking court prevents stormwater runoff, and native landscaping reduces water use for irrigation.

The client arranged donations of all existing fixtures, appliances, and cabinets in good enough condition for reuse to a reclamation organization. Skylights and abundant glazing negate the need for artificial lights throughout the day. Durability of the materials and systems incorporated into the renovation also boosts sustainability by increasing the home's longevity. One of the most important aspects of sustainability is retaining and reimagining an existing house and extending its use for several generations.

SENSITIVE ADDITIONS

Adding on to any structure—especially one with previous alterations—requires thoughtful planning around how the massing will change. Chaotic rooflines can distract from even the best architecture—not to mention the ensuing difficulties during construction.

To create a sense of balance, we essentially matched the original log great room wing and repeated it on the other side of the primary cube, coordinating the length of the pitched roofs (see "Making an addition look right," p. 137). Shortening the existing dormer away from the edges of the

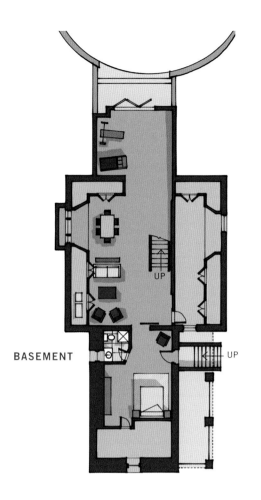

BASEMENT

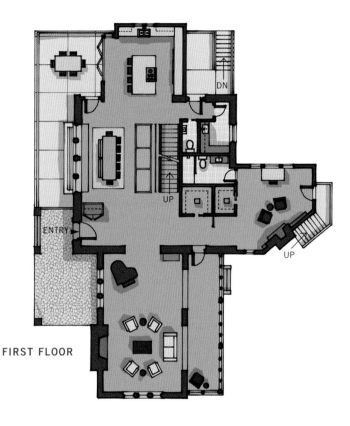

FIRST FLOOR

NORTH ►

CENTERED ON THE STAIRS

The compartmentalized interior of the original plan was extensively reorganized to provide the open concept the homeowners requested. Now, rooms laid out on a strong east-west axis seamlessly connect with each other and are anchored by a feature staircase flooded with light from a skylight above. Each floor feels connected via this shaft of space and light.

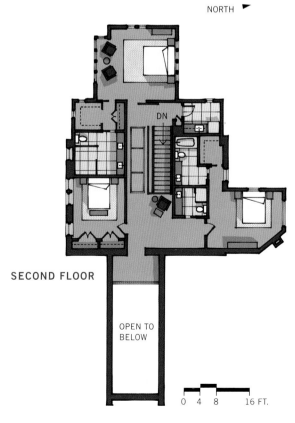

SECOND FLOOR

OPEN TO BELOW

0 4 8   16 FT.

SPECS

Bedrooms: 4

Bathrooms: 6

Size: 3,950 sq. ft

Location: Somerset, Md.

Architect: Bonstra Haresign Architects, bonstra.com

Builder: Thorsen Construction, thorsenconstruction.us

ABOVE AND OPPOSITE: CONTEMPORARY ACCOMMODA-
TIONS. The homeowner cooks for fundraising events
and requested a large-scale dining table. Logs reclaimed
from openings cut out of the original walls now support
dinner for 12 on the 10-ft.-long table.

front-facing gable allowed the dramatic, asymmet-
rical roofline to read more clearly. On the gable end
of the new addition, the end of the south-facing
wall pulls back slightly under the eaves. This move
allows the kitchen and bedroom suite to benefit
from western light while generating a distinctively
modern detail.

Buildings tell you what additions want to be. It's
incumbent on the architect to discover and understand those cues. We separated our intervention
from the original by selecting sympathetic materials and assemblies to contrast and slightly balance

against the historical fabric. For example, cedar planks clad the exterior in homage to the cedar logs, but their vertical placement reads modern. Oversize window walls respect the scale and detail of historical divided-lite casement windows while remaining contemporary.

Renovating an older house with more than one incongruous alteration over the years presented the design team with challenges—as well as highlights. One benefit involved giving a new architect on staff experience in all parts of the process, from permitting to design review presentations to project management throughout construction. Working with a client as enthusiastic and open as this one also provided opportunities to solve functional hurdles through inventive ideas.

Meeting this client's initial goals was a great thing, but I also think we changed the way the family lives in a positive way. The renovated house serves their extensive entertaining needs, but it also feels comfortable when the family is alone. Our client lives in the house where she grew up and loves the transformation. It has become a generational family treasure.

BRAND-NEW OLD BARN

This 17th-century barn with reclaimed materials retains an old feel while including modern features

BY JANICE ROHLF

WHEN THEY DECIDED TO ADD A RUSTIC MODERN barn to their rural property in New Canaan, Conn., the clients returned to architect Mark P. Finlay, with whom they had worked on their main home and garage. The new structure, used mainly as a multigenerational entertaining space, is intended to adapt as the family with five children grows and ages. The relaxing retreat replaced a 17th-century barn whose spirit lives on thanks to a thoughtful selection of building materials—a vintage reclaimed timber frame procured sustainably and set by New Energy Works, which also provided the wall-enclosure system, and reclaimed barnwood supplied by Pioneer Millworks, a sister company of New Energy Works.

The two-story structure includes a kitchen with basin sink, undercounter fridge, and floating Lucite shelving; a double-height living room; and a lofted sitting area. Against the rustic backdrop with raw-timber Craftsman joints, the juxtaposition of sleek materials, like stainless-steel wire railings, is notably pleasing instead of jarring. Symmetrical and oversized black steel window frames provide a sightline through the entire building, and deep-blue barn doors, an accent that connects the restored barn with the main house and garage, are suspended on a track and fully open and close.

Architect: Mark P. Finlay Architects, markfinlay.com
Builder: Hobbs, Inc., hobbsinc.com
Location: New Canaan, Conn.
Photos: Jane Beiles Photography

SUSTAINABLE MOUNTAIN HOME

Construction
that emphasizes
sustainability
and livability
while keeping
to a tight
budget is foun-
dational to this
mining-town
community

BY JANICE ROHLF

CREEDE AMERICA IS A SMALL COMMUNITY OF modest-size houses nestled in Colorado's San Juan Mountains. In homage to the town of Creede's mining history, the architecture nods to the regional vernacular while bringing a definite freshness and modernity to the homes, which range in size between 850 sq. ft. and 3000 sq. ft. Construction that emphasizes sustainability and livability while keeping to a tight budget is foundational to the community. Windows afford natural cross ventilation, and since the cold winters require tightly insulated houses, there is a heat-recovery ventilator (HRV)—common to every Creede America residence—that moves fresh air through the house when doors and windows are closed. Design-wise, each house has special elements that set it apart from the others.

This project, a builder-owner design collaboration, uses plywood for the interior paneling, kitchen, ceiling, and window popout. Instead of full 4x8 sheets for the ceiling, a size that would have been off-scale for the house, the pieces were cut in quarters, and to accentuate the space between the sheets of plywood there is a consistent ¼-in. gap.

Architect/builder: Avery Augur and Jaimi Baer, Caldera Design Build, creedeamerica.com
Location: Creede, Colo.
Photos: Charles Davis Smith, FAIA

RESTORING A HISTORICAL CABIN

This new build incorporates an 1800s log cabin that was painstakingly restored to resemble the original structure

BY JANICE ROHLF

THE ARCHITECTS CALL THIS 1800s LOG CABIN assimilated into a new English country–style house "the tail that wagged the dog." When the homeowners purchased the five-acre property, they were unaware of the cabin's presence, hidden from view behind overgrown shrubbery and a 1925 brick house that was subsequently razed. Discovering the cabin, the architects recognized its historical and architectural significance and were adamant about saving the structure without compromising its authenticity. The homeowners, both history buffs, agreed. A painstaking restoration included replacing rotted logs at the base of the cabin with new wood that was burned and chipped to make it look old.

Left completely in situ, the log cabin was re-chinked, the roof restructured, one elevation rebuilt, and all the windows replaced. Inside, the original low roof was raised, resulting in a space-enhancing cathedral ceiling. Newly insulated, it has become a much-used family room as well as a place to host guests in front of the original fireplace brought back into working order. A glass hallway set at an angle connects the cabin to the house's central vaulted great room.

Architect: BarnesVanze Architects,
barnesvanze.com
Builder: CarrMichael Construction,
carrmichaelconstruction.com
Location: Vienna, Va.
Photos: Anice Hoachlander

THE CABIN CONCEPT

This home
in northern
Idaho puts
savvy space
planning and
craftsmanship
on display
while offering
an alternative
to conventional
home building

BY EMORY BALDWIN

A FEW YEARS AGO, I REALIZED THERE HAD BEEN a shift in the housing needs of Seattle, where I've been designing homes for 16 years. It became clear to me that we needed to create new housing options to address our rapidly changing community. At the time, much of the housing in western Washington did not adequately support an increase in live-in elderly relatives, caregivers, and unrelated adults. Single-person households and multigenerational households were on the rise, while traditional nuclear-family households were declining. An aging population also meant a greater number of people with physical disabilities. Unfortunately, conventional housing options generally do not respond to needs such as these, so I committed myself to designing homes that did.

I started a firm called FabCab, which designs and sells small prefab houses to be used as accessory dwelling units (ADUs), cabin getaways, and primary homes. The houses we produce are designed to be appropriate for a wide range of people with various abilities and to be resource efficient through their low energy demands, their longevity of use, and their compact footprints. Not surprisingly, our clients have been attracted to these homes for those very characteristics, but also because the homes help to foster a comfortable and low-maintenance lifestyle.

Such was the case for the owners of this cabin, who hired Idaho-based contractor Scott Schriber to build the 550-sq.-ft. house we call TimberCab onto the west-facing slope of their steep site, which overlooks Bottle Bay on Lake Pend Oreille.

This home makes use of every square inch of floor space and is designed to feel like and to function as a much larger home. The design strategies we employed are not exclusive to this project but, rather, can be easily adapted to any small home where the goal is to achieve comfort and efficiency in a casual and contemporary style.

A PARTIAL PREFAB

One of the most notable elements of this cabin is its construction. A timber-frame skeleton and a series of structural insulated panels (SIPs) for the walls and roof were cut in a factory and delivered to the site ready to assemble. The shell of the house was flat-packed, meaning that it could be delivered to the site in a much smaller package than a typical modular home, which leaves the factory fully finished and travels down the highway as a volume that is mostly air. Flat-packing the shell proved to be a major benefit in the construction of this house, due to the complicated site access.

A STRATEGIC LAYOUT

With its seating bench and closet, the north entry of the cabin functions like a mudroom. It is placed opposite the home's bathroom, which is far larger than you would expect in a home of this size. The great room features an important bump-out. This shallow projection creates a couch space that defines the living area. The sole bedroom sits at the far end of the house behind a pair of simple sliding barn doors.

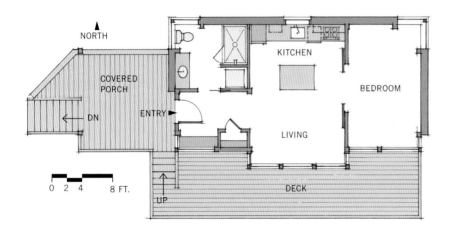

NORTH

COVERED PORCH

DN

ENTRY ►

KITCHEN

BEDROOM

LIVING

DECK

UP

0 2 4   8 FT.

SPECS

Bedrooms: 1
Bathrooms: 1
Cost: $300 per sq. ft.,
    including site work
Completed: 2012
Location: Sagle, Idaho
Architect: Emory Baldwin,
    FabCab, fabcab.com
Builder: Scott Schriber, Selle
    Valley Construction,
    sellevalley.com

550 SQ. FT.

In addition to the timber frame and the SIPs, the house shell includes windows, exterior doors, siding, and roofing. Once the foundation was ready, the timber-frame components were delivered and then assembled without the need for any on-site milling. Tongue-and-groove Douglas-fir planks were installed on top of the timber rafters to create a finished ceiling and to provide a solid walking surface for installing the SIP roof panels. The intent was for the shell to be built in as little as two weeks, including the installation of the windows and doors, so that it could be dried in quickly.

Not only did the prefabrication expedite construction, but the resulting home is tight and well insulated—R-25 walls and an R-40 roof—which allows it to be conditioned by a single ductless-minisplit heat pump. The cabin's owners also opted for radiant-floor heating in the bathroom, though primarily for comfort.

MODERN DESIGN, TRADITIONAL COMFORT

I would describe the design of this home as a marriage of modern aesthetics and traditional materials. The monoslope shed roof, large expanses of glass, and simple form are far more contemporary elements than those on the gable-roofed cabins and cottages typical of the area. Yet this home's use of time-honored timber-frame construction and its abundance of wood inside and out create an environment imbued with a sense of warmth that few people associate with modern design. The prolific use of Douglas fir and engineered oak flooring also helps to make the cabin feel in harmony with its mountainous location, heavily timbered valleys, and shoreline.

The few other details in the house—such as the large sculptural light fixtures and the stainless-steel door hardware and tile backsplash—round out the home's contrasting yet complementary styles.

SMART SMALL-SPACE FEATURES

Although this home has an unusually compact footprint, it was designed to provide a living experience without compromising comfort or convenience. Nowhere is that design approach more evident than in the home's interior spaces. Here, several design strategies are used to support an ordinary lifestyle, albeit at a reduced scale.

COMPOUNDING TASKS. In an effort to make the most of every square foot, a recess for a bench was created in the entry and wrapped in windows. This simple detail allows the entry to function as a mudroom or a space to hole up with a book.

SPACE DECEPTION. The central living area seems far larger than it is due to a fully exposed Douglas-fir ceiling that rises toward the view. Windows wrap a small projection to increase daylight access and to lengthen the sightlines through the house.

"Selectively giving a small home big-house spaces has an important impact on how well the home lives."

COMPACT GALLEY. A slender 24-in. Liebherr fridge and freezer anchors one end of the prep zone, which is topped with Stormy Sky honed quartz. An induction cooktop is placed at the other. The homeowners chose additional storage over a conventional oven in this small kitchen. The custom steel-and-slab table serves as a dining area and as an additional prep surface, and it allows the kitchen and living area to be somewhat flexible in size.

CREATING EXPANSIVE QUALITIES

With this house, an enhanced sense of space was achieved through several design decisions. For instance, the layout of the cabin is anchored by a great room that contains the living area as well as a combined dining space and galley kitchen. The bedroom, bathroom, and entry are organized around this core. Having the largest open space at the center of the cabin, with other spaces opening onto it, gives the entire home a more spacious feel. The idea of a central core is an organizing element in every iteration of our stock designs (see "Prefab expandable," p. 154).

High ceilings and clear space above the few partition walls allow the entire ceiling to be visible, which highlights the home's complete volume and contributes to its spacious feel. The ceiling rises toward the view, and a wall of windows captures it, maximizing the sightlines throughout the house—a common small-home design strategy that increases the perception of space—while also providing the house with an abundance of natural light.

Among the most significant spaces of the house are its patio and deck, which expand its livable footprint when weather allows. Part of the stock design, the covered patio serves as both a covered

PREFAB EXPANDABLE

FabCab offers five standard versions of its TimberCab design. If more space is needed, the four additional layouts provide additional square footage rooted in the same design logic as the 550-sq.-ft. plan.

982 SQ. FT.

This plan adds a second bedroom or flex space, which mirrors the primary bedroom on the other side of the living area. The kitchen is expanded to add a small island, and the living and dining areas are stretched slightly.

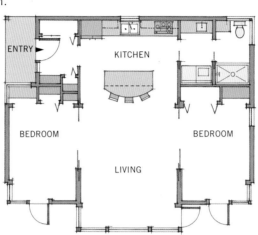

1,226 SQ. FT.

This plan includes a master suite and adds a dedicated laundry room and guest bathroom adjacent to a second bedroom. The kitchen, dining, and living areas are expanded, and the entrance is moved to the low (nonview) side of the home.

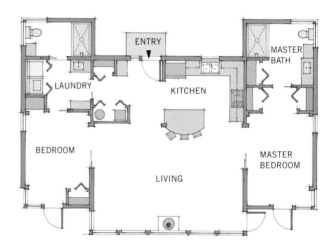

1,485 SQ. FT.

This plan has two bedrooms, a den or flex space, and two full bathrooms. A walk-in closet and mudroom are added near the entry, and the kitchen is larger and now situated on the view side of the home. The largest plan is 1,850 sq. ft. and has the same layout as this plan, but its spaces are increased in size proportionally.

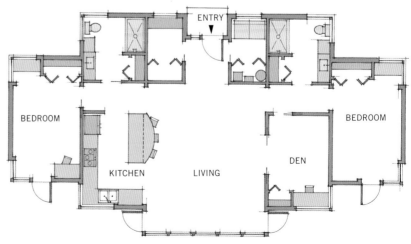

MOUNTAIN MODERN. The best way to connect a home with its setting is to construct it of native materials and create spaces to interact with it. This small home celebrates those ideals with a natural palette of exterior finishes; Douglas-fir beams, siding, and decking; and a carefully designed deck and patio.

entry and an outdoor dining space. The addition of the generous deck was a collaboration between Schriber and the homeowners. It is an ideal area for entertaining and relaxing. Wisely, the deck—which helps ground the house to its site—is dropped well below the windows of the house, creating uninterrupted views of the lake and mountains

BROAD APPLICABILITY

When I first designed this home, I couldn't have foreseen it being built in the rugged country of northern Idaho. Additionally, the nature of our

firm's work usually keeps us fairly removed from the build, especially when it's a flight away. But when we do get to visit projects upon their completion, I always find it to be rewarding. For me, designing any home has its challenges, but designing a small home with the hopes of it serving a variety of clients in a range of settings has been particularly daunting. Yet through successful projects like this one, our effort to create quality, broadly applicable homes that help enrich the lives of those who live in them is affirmed.

A REMARKABLE HOME REMODEL

Turning a quirky rustic lodge into a comfortable modern home is a problem-solving proposition

BY BRIAN PONTOLILO

ABOUT 100 YEARS AGO, AN UNKNOWN FISHERMAN built a quirky stone lodge on the banks of the Colorado River outside Austin, Texas. Over time, the house and the city both grew. The house acquired a series of unbecoming additions. The city ultimately encircled the once-remote riverside property.

For many, the value of the lodge would not have been the anomalous structure but its location in a desirable commuter neighborhood. This project could easily have been a tear-down. But homeowner Steve Luning saw it differently. Steve had just visited Spain, where he was struck by the seamless integration of modern details into very old buildings. Not only did he admire the charm of the rustic old home, but he also saw the potential to modernize the house in a similar way.

To get the job done, Steve put together a stellar team—including Furman + Keil Architects, RisherMartin Fine Homes, and Mark Word Design—to help with the landscape plan and implementation. Even with decades of combined experience and talent, though, the team was challenged by site restrictions, structural irregularities, and, ultimately, the complexity of executing their own design.

AN ENIGMATIC BUILDING

The original lodge was a seemingly simple structure with a cross-gable form. Like many old homes, a couple of additions were tacked on over the years as the owners needed more space. With design and construction said and done, the scope of work for this remodel could be seen as removing, redesigning, and rebuilding the additions while keeping the original cottage's form and character. But that would be a gross oversimplification of all that the design and build teams accomplished.

BEFORE

AFTER

DURING

MONOLITHIC MASONRY. The home's original walls, built with stone likely collected nearby, extend below grade to act as their own foundation. The owner wanted to keep as much of the walls intact as possible to retain the old-fishing-lodge charm. In the end, however, much of the walls would need to be rebuilt to repair a number of conditions and correct their odd original construction

LEFT, BELOW, AND OPPOSITE:
RADIANT TEXTURE. The existing
stone chimney, with its Viking head
and unfinished Nordic epitaph,
was converted to a gas fireplace.
The interior design is a balance of
rustic texture and clean lines—the
former created with details like
the herringbone-pattern flooring,
wire-brushed cabinetry, and glass-
tile backsplash; the latter achieved
with modern details like the drywall
returns in place of window and door
casings, the flat-panel cabinetry
style, and the steel-framed
dining-room ceiling.

No one is quite sure when the lodge was built or who built it. The stone is believed to have been collected from the river, and the masonry work was likely part of an amateur, owner-built project. The original stone walls, which extend below grade to act as the foundation, varied in thickness from one to the next. And the gables were not even close to square. Though some of each original gable wall stayed intact, much of what looks original was rebuilt to repair a range of problematic conditions.

As Jeremy Martin, one of the principals at Risher Martin, put it, "This project had more problems per square foot than we'd ever seen." If the unusual structure wasn't enough, the site had a municipal drainage easement running through it and three Heritage live oaks, trees protected by the city above and below ground. If the project hadn't been a remodel, it would have been nearly impossible to squeeze a new home into the lot and meet current zoning regulations.

AN ECLECTIC STYLE

Though the remodel earned a five-star rating from the Austin Energy Green Building program, Philip Keil, who led the design team, says that they didn't think too much about achieving a particular designation. "We didn't make decisions based on points," he said. "We made our decisions to make sure we were building the best house for Steve."

Philip describes the floor plan, interior design, and new exterior elevations of the house as an arrangement of public and private spaces. The public living spaces are arranged within the footprint of the original cabin. Some of the supporting spaces—the powder room, pantry, and studio—are in an addition on the back of the house, which also includes the homeowner's daily entry and mudroom. The bedrooms and office are in another addition on the opposite side, which is set at an angle to the lodge to follow the property line and maximize the size of the house.

While the interior design takes many of its cues from the original lodge, particularly the stone fireplace, it has modern elements too. For example, the white-oak flooring is set in a herringbone

pattern and the white-oak cabinetry has a wire-brush finish, both chosen to carry the rich texture of the fireplace around the interior. The steel hand-rail in the entry, the steel-framed dining-room ceiling, and the plaster returns at the windows and doors give the house clean, modern lines.

Philip describes a similar approach to the exterior elevations, noting three specific features that make it work: the original stone gable walls; three new bump-outs for the main entry, dining room, and bedroom; and the stucco walls of the additions. The existing masonry walls maintain the character and shape of the lodge. The modern steel-and-glass bump-outs have a furniture-like quality. And

the stucco walls provide a subtle backdrop for the old stone walls and new modern boxes.

AN EFFORT FOR THE AGES

RisherMartin is a fixed-price contractor; they provide a firm price for each project before construction begins. This means they do a lot of work leading up to construction. For Chris Risher, Jeremy's partner, the most exceptional part of this project was the collaboration between their firm, the architects, and the landscape designers. From design and preconstruction documentation to rebuilding the home and installing the hardscape, the team tackled each challenge together.

OPPOSITE AND ABOVE: DEMOLITION DERBY. Though most of the original lodge was demolished, the remodeled house maintains a similar footprint that meets zoning setback regulations and protects the site's Heritage live oak trees. The bedroom addition is angled to the rest of the home to squeeze in a little extra space—the new home is about 100 sq. ft. larger than before the remodel. The landscape plan includes similarly patterned concrete and steel retaining walls used to terrace the grade. The garage siding detail mimics the retaining walls.

Construction photos from the project reveal a ruinlike job site with three partial stone walls standing tall while the crew shores them up with shotcrete—sprayed concrete commonly used for pools—and pours new slab foundations for the additions. The lodge proper is built above a sealed crawlspace. The floors are framed like a deck, with ledgers hung on the masonry walls, now flattened by the shotcrete. The team decided to lower the height of the new slab foundations of the additions and frame the floors with sleepers so the finished floors have a similar feel to the wood-framed floors above the crawlspace.

Spraying the masonry walls with shotcrete also provided an opportunity to square the walls— inside the home, at least. Outside, the walls are still not square.

The team engineered a new structural steel fascia—a continuous header, really—that runs along the eaves and rakes of the masonry walls and helps to hide their imperfections. Philip explains that steel fascia solves a couple of problems: "The projecting horizontal steel plate at the top of the stone acts as 'trim' to clean up the edge of the stone, which was very rough and out of square. The vertical leg of the fascia adds height to the wall, raising the ceiling in what was originally a very low space. The fascia profile also creates a shadow line at the top of the wall that emphasizes the shape of the structure and contrasts with the thin edge of the metal roof."

Though Philip describes the simplicity of the home's design, many of the materials were chosen for problem-solving reasons. Austin has a hot and humid climate, for example, so the team expected regular moisture migration through the masonry walls. While they used a liquid-applied vapor barrier on all of the new walls, they chose to manage the effect of moisture movement in the masonry walls instead of trying to stop its passage.

The team chose steel windows for the masonry walls, though they used wood windows in the new walls. They decided to use plaster instead of drywall for its natural durability and laid a limestone border around the perimeter of the interior to keep the wood flooring away from any moisture making its way through the masonry walls. In the additions, the mechanicals run in conditioned attic space. In the original home, the mechanicals run through the crawlspace. And the mechanical systems include a dedicated dehumidifier, now considered best practice in this climate and particularly important in this home.

Even the landscape, designed by Sarah Carr, a principal at Mark Word Design, had to solve problems. Specifically, the retaining walls that were planned to terrace the sloping site couldn't obstruct access to a city drainage system that runs beneath the lot. The city accepted Sarah's steel walls as an easily removable compromise. Sarah aligned the welds in the steel wall with bands in the board-formed concrete walls used elsewhere—delicate concrete bands that Jeremy and the concrete contractor struggled to figure out how not to break when removing the concrete forms. And finally, as if this project weren't challenging enough, the team decided to align the welds and the bands with the reveals in the garage's open rainscreen siding on the other side of the driveway.

SPECS

Bedrooms: 2
Bathrooms: 2½
Size before: 2,071 sq. ft.
Size after: 2,183 sq. ft.
Completed: 2016
Location: Austin, Texas
Architect: Furman + Keil Architects, fkarchitects.net
Builder: RisherMartin Fine Homes, rishermartin.com
Landscape Design: Mark Word Design, markworddesign.com

BEFORE

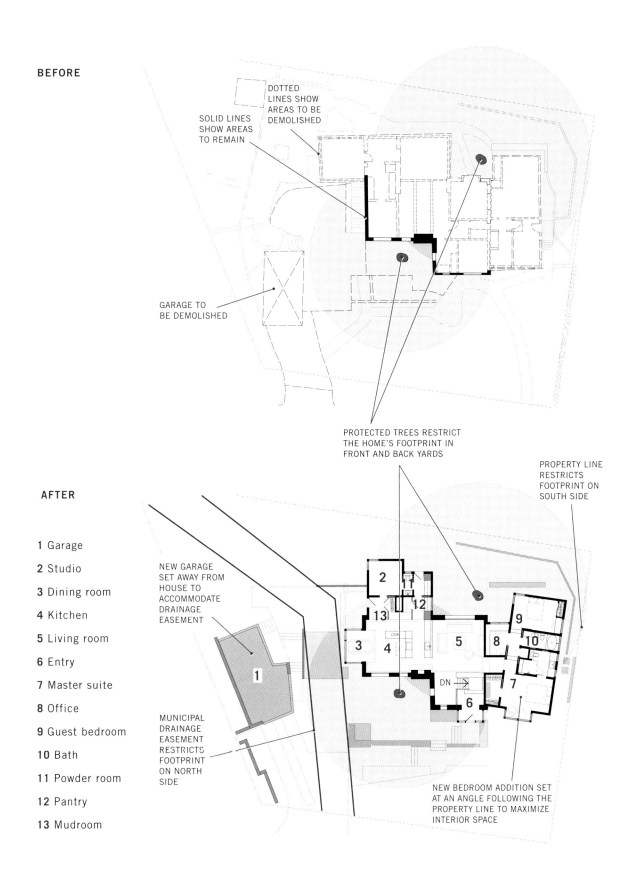

DOTTED LINES SHOW AREAS TO BE DEMOLISHED

SOLID LINES SHOW AREAS TO REMAIN

GARAGE TO BE DEMOLISHED

PROTECTED TREES RESTRICT THE HOME'S FOOTPRINT IN FRONT AND BACK YARDS

PROPERTY LINE RESTRICTS FOOTPRINT ON SOUTH SIDE

AFTER

1 Garage

2 Studio

3 Dining room

4 Kitchen

5 Living room

6 Entry

7 Master suite

8 Office

9 Guest bedroom

10 Bath

11 Powder room

12 Pantry

13 Mudroom

NEW GARAGE SET AWAY FROM HOUSE TO ACCOMMODATE DRAINAGE EASEMENT

MUNICIPAL DRAINAGE EASEMENT RESTRICTS FOOTPRINT ON NORTH SIDE

NEW BEDROOM ADDITION SET AT AN ANGLE FOLLOWING THE PROPERTY LINE TO MAXIMIZE INTERIOR SPACE

DN

MAGNIFICENT MOUNTAIN CABIN

Designed to tread lightly on the land and with minimal amenities, this family retreat is still built to last

BY ROB WOTZAK

TWO GENERATIONS OF MAGGIE AND RON'S FAMILY live on a rural property in northern Vermont, and it's not unusual for four generations to visit at a time. This small cabin, located on a remote corner of the family land, is a favorite place for everyone. At times it serves as a guest house for friends, and the couple also hosts parties there. Maggie and Ron are especially pleased that it fulfills their original objective as a private retreat, free from the distractions of the modern world. They envisioned it as a place to take breaks from their busy work lives, where they could curl up with a good book, warm themselves by the woodstove on a cool evening, or just sit and take in the beautiful view.

As purposeful as this all sounds, it was actually a random act of nature that precipitated the cabin's conception. While working on an overall landscape plan for the family property, garden designer Ed Burke discovered that a stand of white pine trees had blown down and revealed a panoramic view of a nearby mountain range. He suggested that a screened-in lean-to would be a perfect addition—a structure that would sit lightly on the site and allow Maggie and Ron to enjoy the rugged clearing and the spectacular vista it created.

Ed enlisted the help of his husband, Boston architect David Flaschenriem, to design the simple building. As the designers and homeowners worked on ideas for the project, the concept grew from a simple shed for keeping out rain and mosquitoes into a cabin that could comfortably accommodate guests throughout the year. But they held fast to their commitment to creating a place with few amenities and one that required little maintenance.

Because the best views are to the southwest, David came up with a clever plan. He designed most of the structure parallel to the main axis of the hillside, but turned the angle of the south- and east-facing walls 10° to face the view. Aligning the cedar decking and soffit boards with these walls adds a sense of movement to the design.

Maggie and Ron wanted to retain as much of the native landscape as possible, and a pier foundation seemed to be the least invasive solution. But with two-dozen piers needed, building the foundation was no simple task. Though it took a fraction of the concrete needed for a basement or crawlspace, the piers required nearly as much excavation as a typical foundation to make room for the site-built forms and to get everything deep enough to stay put through Vermont's winter frost. And it was no small feat to plumb and level the forms so each pier lines up perfectly with its corresponding point on the complex floor framing.

DECKED OUT. To make as little impact as possible on the mountainside landscape while capturing the stunning view across the valley, this family cabin is built on piers and navigates the sloped site with a ramp, a wraparound deck, and a boardwalk from the cabin to the outhouse.

OUT OF SQUARE, ON PURPOSE

While the roof, deck, and north- and west-facing walls are all aligned with and square to the hillside slope, the south- and east-facing walls are set at an angle. Though they were designed to maximize views, these angled walls add lots of visual interest to the cabin. In this way, each aspect of the design is either functional or intended to accentuate the unique modern aesthetic.

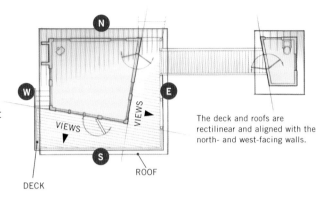

The deck and roofs are rectilinear and aligned with the north- and west-facing walls.

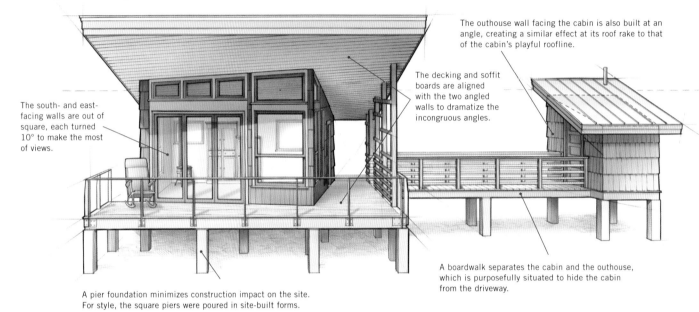

The south- and east-facing walls are out of square, each turned 10° to make the most of views.

The outhouse wall facing the cabin is also built at an angle, creating a similar effect at its roof rake to that of the cabin's playful roofline.

The decking and soffit boards are aligned with the two angled walls to dramatize the incongruous angles.

A boardwalk separates the cabin and the outhouse, which is purposefully situated to hide the cabin from the driveway.

A pier foundation minimizes construction impact on the site. For style, the square piers were poured in site-built forms.

VERMONT TRADITIONS. The builder used random-width boards recycled from a 19th-century house for paneling on the ceiling. The cabin's owners picked transparent yellow milk paint to showcase the grain of the rough-sawn shiplap wall paneling.

NATURAL CEDAR AND PAINTED PINE. The decking and trim is all unfinished white cedar, which will age to a natural gray color. The unusually tall 20-in. painted shingles were hand-cut on site from white-pine slabs.

SANDBLASTED STEEL. The east and west sides of the deck have white-cedar railings. On the south-facing side, a stainless-steel cable railing exposes the view. The builder sandblasted the railing to remove its sheen.

The grid of concrete columns ended up looking taller than expected. It took a fair amount of fill and boulders to soften the transition between the house and the existing topography, but once Ed flanked the cabin with native plants and shrubs, the construction site quickly began to blend back into its wild surroundings. Though the look of the cabin is strikingly modern, the muted colors and matte finishes also help it blend in with the surrounding trees and rocks.

Salvaged lumber from old barns and farmhouses and locally milled timber are abundant in Vermont. Aside from the stone hearth and the metal roof and railings, every visible surface is made of these materials. The roof is the cabin's flashiest detail, but standing-seam roofs are common in Vermont because of their excellent snow-shedding qualities.

Even though this is a simple cabin, which only occasionally needs heat from the Vermont Castings woodstove, the builders—Smith & McClain of Bristol, Vt.—didn't skimp on the comfort and weatherization details. After filling the floor, walls, and ceiling with mineral-wool batt insulation, they covered the interior framing with Intello Plus, a smart vapor retarder. To further keep moisture at bay, they wrapped the exterior sheathing with Benjamin Obdyke's Slicker HP, a good match for the pine shingles.

There's no running water in the cabin, but a large rain barrel captures runoff from the roof to be used for cleaning tasks and to water plants. And to make the cabin comfortable for extended visits, there's a Sun-Mar composting toilet in a small building across the deck, which Maggie dubbed "La Poopière"—presumably to make it sound more inviting to outhouse-averse guests.

After some deliberation, Maggie and Ron did opt for an electrical hookup to power lights and a ceiling fan, but they believe they could do without electricity because they tend to use candles as their primary lighting.

It may seem odd to design and build such a refined little abode while simultaneously working so hard to omit most of the conveniences many of us demand in our own homes. But this rustic retreat works exactly the way the couple intended. As Maggie puts it, "I don't feel as if we have given up a thing—this cabin is a luxury to me because of what it allows us to do and experience."

FROM CABIN TO HIGH-PERFORMANCE HOME

A cabin is transformed into a high-performance home that highlights the structure's original framing

BY KILEY JACQUES

WHAT BEGAN AS A DARK, OLD BARN-TURNED-hunting cabin is now a light-filled high-performance home. The idea was to celebrate the framing structure, pay homage to the building's history, and better its overall performance.

In the kitchen, subway tile lends a classic look, but bringing it up to the ceiling—beneath and above the beams—gives it a modern feel and calls attention to the framing. The original stairs were relocated, and the second-floor loft was reconfigured to allow for two small bedrooms and a bathroom. The middle room is centered on the window, which was enlarged, and on the peak of the gable roof. A beam crosses in front of the newly enlarged window in yet another effort to highlight the old barn structure.

Designer: Bluetime Collaborative, bluetimecollaborative.com
Interior Designer: Joanne Palmisano Design, joannepalmisano.com
Builder: Webster Construction and Helm Construction Solutions, buildhelm.com
Location: Southern Vermont
Photos: Lindsay Selin Photography, lindsayselinphotography.com

DOWNSIZE AND SIMPLIFY

This compact near-zero-energy home is designed for those looking to live well with minimal impact

BY ROB YAGID

IN MANY WAYS, NICO AND ELLEN ARE NOT UNLIKE others of their generation. Years ago, they worked hard to buy a house in downtown Freeport, Maine, where they could settle and raise a family. They did so, bringing up three children in a charming old village Victorian that needed and received lots of work over the years. The family grew together in that house, and then their kids got older and went off to college and on to lives of their own. As empty-nesters, Nico and Ellen were left with a house larger than they needed and, subsequently, with energy bills and a maintenance list larger than they wanted. They had arrived at the moment where many other baby boomers have found themselves, or soon will: Their home no longer fit the life they lived.

This wasn't a surprise. Nico and Ellen had been dreaming of downsizing and of living in a house as considerate of the earth's resources as they were. That meant building a small, low-energy, and low-maintenance home. They had already purchased a lot a couple of miles outside of town on a bluff above the Cousins River, a meandering tidal river that brings abundant wildlife and the qualities of the coast they love so much right to the fringe of their property. They restored a meadow that had been overtaken by forest, and in the middle of it they built a 1,600-sq.-ft., modern, near-zero-energy home tuned to its environment and to the next chapter of their lives.

Looking at this new home designed and built by the Maine firm GO Logic, you are confronted with a carefully considered design that is both smart and sensible. The home's basic form, pared-down details, limited material palette, and inviting, naturally lit living spaces evoke a comfortable, modern style. And though it departs from a conventionally built house in many ways, none of it is overly complicated or out of reach. You may very well allow yourself to think, "I can build that."

You would be absolutely right. You can—and here is how.

BE INSPIRED BY DESIGN IN ALL ITS FORMS

Nico and Ellen had first seen GO Logic's work on the cover of a regional design magazine. The GO Home, one of the firm's first projects, was a small LEED-Platinum-certified Passive House. The couple fell in love with the home's style and its performance. The aspects of its design mirrored how they were hoping to live. They sought the firm out, despite having already talked to another potential builder.

Nico recalls the initial conversation with principal Matt O'Malia and project architect Gunther Kragler: "When it came to efficiency, which was

NEAR-ZERO ENERGY. This compact Maine home, designed and built by GO Logic, is an example of how contemporary design can be married to exceptional building techniques to create a comfortable, low-impact home within an approachable budget.

SIMPLE IN SHAPE AND PLAN

1 Master bedroom
2 Master bath
3 Bedroom
4 Bath
5 Living
6 Dining
7 Kitchen
8 Porch
9 Deck
10 Covered walkway
11 Garage

SPECS
Bedrooms: 3
Bathrooms: 2
Size: 1,600 sq. ft.
Cost: $215 per sq. ft., excluding site work, walkway, and garage
Completed: 2014
Location: Freeport, Maine
Architect: Matt O'Malia and Gunther Kragler, GO Logic, gologic.us
Builder: Alan Gibson, GO Logic; Isaac Wood

important to us, the first builder seemed to just be adding it onto his standard building package. Matt and Gunther seemed much more knowledgeable, and efficiency seemed completely integrated into the design of their home." Nico and Ellen, though not versed in performance building, recognized something critical in home design during that conversation: Successful homes are designed as systems, and not as sets of disparate parts and assemblies.

GO Logic's strategy is straightforward: Design contemporary houses that are simple in shape and plan, which makes them less costly and easier to build, insulate, and air-seal. The firm allocates a larger than average percentage of a project's budget to the shell of the house—thick, well-insulated

LIVING LIGHTLY. The living room is bookended by a custom ash daybed and accent wall, which is just one of a few touches in the house that denote a Scandinavian style. The room is daylit by a wall of glass doors to the south, and a custom built-in bookcase serves as an important focal point to the north.

walls and roofs, and top-performing windows. This allows for a mechanical system that is greatly reduced in size and complexity, which helps keep the up-front building budget in check while ensuring low long-term operating costs in the way of minimal energy bills.

CHOOSE LOGIC OVER CONVENTION

With GO Logic's general style and performance approach grounding the project, Matt and Gunther asked Nico and Ellen for a list of the features they liked in the homes of their friends and family members. Single-floor living appealed to them, as did a seamless flow between the kitchen and indoor and outdoor living spaces. Though Nico and Ellen would live in their home alone much of the time, it still had to accommodate visitors. These demands guided the siting and layout of the home.

Upon approaching the house, the first element you encounter is the garage. As Gunther acknowledges, "It's not always the most beautiful element, but it helps start an important procession to the entry." Having the garage in such a forward position creates a stark transition between the frenetic pace of the workday and the quiet and peace of home. The garage also provides privacy, and because it's completely detached from the house, it ensures better indoor-air quality.

The front door, accessed by a short walk beneath an elevated covered walkway, sits beyond a sliding wooden screened and slatted door to the porch. This sliding door can be closed in the summer, allowing the front door to be left open, which helps realize Nico and Ellen's desire for seamless indoor and outdoor living when the weather allows.

The floor plan, based on one of GO Logic's stock designs, is basic but hardworking. The master bed-

CASUAL ELEGANCE. The kitchen carries the contemporary styling of the house and is organized for efficiency, storage, and everyday food prep and entertaining. Its openness not only improves the comfort of the kitchen but also that of the adjacent dining and living area.

room, the kitchen, and the dining and living areas are along the southern wall of the house, which has lots of glass for natural daylighting, solar heat gain, and views of the property. All of the compact public spaces sit beneath a continuously vaulted ceiling, which helps make them feel bright and expansive. The guest bedrooms and bathrooms are placed along the north wall. Lowering the ceiling in these areas to a standard height creates attic-storage opportunities above, helps create a chase to run ductwork, and reduces their scale to make them comfortable.

Instead of a partition wall, a custom bookcase divides the home into public and private halves. This unit is made of ash and translucent panels. It provides privacy for the bedrooms and bathroom but allows light to pass through. Beyond its capacity to hold books and art, the unit is an important focal point. At night, the bookcase is set aglow with integrated lighting and translucent panels that become backlit from the hall lights.

EMBRACE BETTER BUILDING

The shell of Nico and Ellen's home exceeds code-minimum construction considerably. The foundation is of GO Logic's own design and is a version of what's commonly called a raft slab. Thick EPS rigid foam is laid like a tray over structural fill. Once poured, the thickened-edge slab is completely isolated from the exterior environment to eliminate thermal bridging that can result in cold, uncomfortable floors and energy losses. The wall assemblies are insulated to R-50 and are made of a 2x6 load-bearing interior wall insulated with dense-pack cellulose and an outer wall made of 8¼-in.-thick structural insulated panels (SIPs).

The roof is framed primarily with trusses that accommodate 2 ft. of loose-fill cellulose to provide an insulating value in excess of R-80. With triple-glazed aluminum-clad Kneer-Süd windows and doors, the home's conditioning needs are so low that the primary heat comes from just a few small and inexpensive electric baseboard heaters. A fresh-air supply—imperative in such an airtight, well-insulated home—is provided by a Zehnder

ABOVE AND RIGHT: AN EFFICIENT, BEAUTIFUL FORM. The home's simple shape and peaked shed roofs lend efficiency in energy performance and cost, and its materials speak to regional influences. Clapboard siding and pine timbers used to construct the walkway and porch are just a few of the subtle details that make this project at home on its site.

heat-recovery ventilator (HRV) that exhausts stale air from the kitchen and two bathrooms and introduces fresh air to the living room and bedrooms. There is no need for air-conditioning in the summer months. The simple, all-electric mechanical system is supported by a 4.6kw photovoltaic array, which helps keep the annual heating costs at just $300.

The final components of the mechanical system are the water heaters. To reduce energy use and utility costs, two 40-gal. electric water heaters were installed. When just Nico and Ellen are home, one heater keeps up with the demand. When guests arrive, flipping a switch activates the second unit.

Such smart strategies set this home apart from most others. Nico, who may not have recognized the truth in that statement before building this house, has a whole new perspective and a new

message. "If you're building a new house, you totally owe it to yourself to find a builder who knows what's possible with today's building materials and technology," he says. "Now, when I drive by what seems to be a typical build, one that looks like it's being built to the basic code, it just seems like such a wasted opportunity."

We can build better, and this particular home in Maine's midcoast region is a testament to what's possible when a designer, a builder, and their clients are guided by building science's best practices and a commitment to true quality in design.

RIGHT SIZED ON A TIGHT LOT

An architect designs a right-sized, certified Platinum home on a challenging building lot in British Columbia

BY JAMES TUER

THERE IS TRUTH TO THE SAYING THAT ARCHITECTS are only as good as their clients. The best clients challenge you. They are inspired and informed. Their projects have limitations, yet they're not willing to settle for anything less than a house that truly reflects their lifestyle and their values. Lauren and Kevin were these kinds of clients. They came to me with a clear vision: to build a house that would lead the way in sustainable design and construction in the rock-climbing mecca of Squamish, British Columbia. Lauren and Kevin wanted to demonstrate that it is possible to build a healthy, efficient, and comfortable family home that isn't any larger than necessary, and to do it without sacrificing functionality.

From our first meeting, Lauren and Kevin had a list of must-haves for their project. Their list included a bedroom and full bath on the first floor, two additional bedrooms, space for a home office, storage for their climbing gear, a sociable front porch, and a generous garden to grow their own food. Lauren and Kevin were well-versed in the small house movement, so they knew that with good design, their must-haves were all possible. Healthy indoor air quality was also non-negotiable. They specifically did not want any materials that would off-gas or contaminate their house with allergens or polutants. Perhaps surprisingly, renewable energy wasn't on the list (this is a relatively low-tech home).

When we met, Lauren and Kevin had already purchased a 33-ft. by 120-ft. lot with a grassy laneway in the back and a wonderful view of Penny Lane, one of Squamish's choice rock-climbing routes. It was an infill lot between two existing homes with a bus stop directly in front (both would offer us points toward LEED certification, something we would later decide to pursue). Though Squamish frowns on small lots and theirs was 2 ft. short of the minimum width, we were able to apply for a hardship and managed to get a variance as the existing lot had sat vacant for years, waiting for the right people to recognize its value. Not only did we successfully manage to build a 1,200-sq.-ft. house on the site, the landscape plan includes container and in-ground gardens where Lauren and Kevin can grow their food (more LEED points).

A TWIST ON TRADITION. Like the front porch on so many homes, this outdoor space is meant to be inviting, charming, and cozy, but not at the expense of daylighting and warming the house. For this reason, the porch roof was kept back from the corner windows and has two large skylights that allow light to reach the living room inside.

SECOND FLOOR

NORTH

THE POTENTIAL FOR SINGLE-FLOOR LIVING

There are a few key principles to making a small home work. One is to keep the spaces as open as possible, and another is to extend the indoor spaces to the outdoors. This home has an open living area on the first floor, with the living room connected to the front porch and the kitchen connected to the back deck. With a bedroom, full bath, and laundry also on the first floor, the home is designed for the possibility of single-floor living. Upstairs are two additional bedrooms and another full bath, plus open spaces to be used as a play space or home office.

SPECS
Bedrooms: 3
Bathrooms: 3
Size: 1,200 sq. ft.
Cost: $312 per sq. ft.
Completed: 2014
Location: Squamish, B.C.
Architect: James Tuer, JWT Architecture, jwtarchitecture.com
Builder: Ray Dierolf, Westerncraft Contracting, westerncraftcontracting.ca

FIRST FLOOR

THE SEARCH FOR LIGHT AND VIEWS

A big part of designing a house for an infill lot is creating privacy without completely turning away from sunlight and while still connecting to the outdoors. This was particularly important here, in one of the most scenic cities in Canada. In just about every direction there is either a stunning rock face or a distant mountain peak. Though this house is quite traditional at a glance, there are some subtle nontraditional details that make it work with its surroundings.

Though Lauren and Kevin wanted a quintessential front porch, the house faces south, so the front is where it would get the most sunlight to the interior and have the most solar heating potential. We decided to cut the porch roof short of the full width of the house and invite light into the living room with a large corner window. We also put skylights in the porch roof to light the porch itself and to let in more sun to reach and warm the concrete floors inside.

A HEALTHY ENTRANCE

The entry vestibule, with its floor mat and shoe rack, is an important part of a strategy for healthy indoor air quality by offering a place to leave contaminants at the door. Beyond the barn-style sliding door is a utility closet where the adventurous homeowners store their climbing, biking, and other outdoor gear. A single step down signals the entry into the living room, where the home's radiant heating system warms the stained concrete floors and the woodstove offers supplemental heating and ambience. At the beam separating the living and dining rooms, the ceiling finish changes to drywall, defining the space. Here, the bookcase stairway takes center stage.

TWO WALLS SHARE A PLATE

Staggered-stud walls are a less common cousin of double-stud walls—both create space for continuous insulation that prevents heat loss through the studs (thermal bridging). Instead of building two separate walls with the studs aligned, however, here the 2x4 studs are staggered every 8 in. on the 2x10 plates, either to the inside or outside face of the plates. In this way, much of the wall has a full 9¼ in. of mineral-wool insulation and even at the studs there is 5¾ in. of continuous insulation and no thermal bridge.

1 2x12 rafters insulated with closed-cell spray foam (unvented roof assembly; approx R-41)

2 Mineral-wool batt insulation (approx. R-37)

3 Tongue-and-groove Douglas-fir floor and finished ceiling

4 Insulated header

5 Exposed Douglas-fir floor framing

6 2x10 top and bottom plates

7 Finished concrete slab with tubing for radiant heat

8 2 in. of EPS rigid insulation creates a thermal break between the slab and stem wall (approx. R-8)

9 6 in. of EPS rigid insulation (approx. R-24)

10 Frost-depth footing

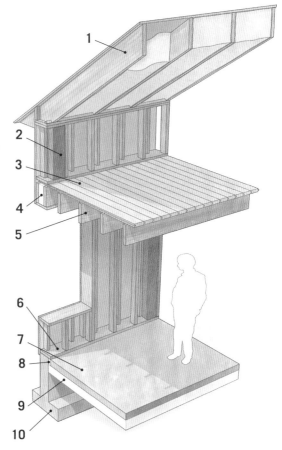

Inside the front door, where the stair would typically be located in a house like this, we put a utility closet. The closet is used to store rock-climbing gear, mountain bikes, and outerwear. The utility closet also serves a second purpose as a space for some of the home's mechanical equipment.

In turn, we located the stair off the kitchen and it became the focal point of the interior. The L-shaped Douglas-fir stair has a sculptural quality with its extra-stout treads, newels, balusters, and built-in shelves beneath the stringers. But these bookshelves are more than decorative—they provide needed storage. Lit from above by a skylight and dormer windows, the stair landing provides a warm perch for sitting and viewing activity in the kitchen from above.

Though the kitchen wall directly faces a neighbor's house, we incorporated long, horizontal windows along the kitchen counter to illuminate the work surface with natural light while still maintaining privacy.

Upstairs, the second-floor hallway wraps around the stair and includes a central nook that can be used for a home office or a play area for kids. On both the east- and west-facing roofs, dormers provide light and mountain views as well as headroom in the bath. Under the gables on the south- and east-facing walls are the two additional bedrooms. At the eaves, attic space is used for mechanicals and more storage.

GOING FOR GOLD, ACHIEVING PLATINUM

From our first meeting, Lauren and Kevin set the bar high with a demanding program for this project. When builder Ray Dierolf joined the team and saw what we were hoping to achieve, he suggested

that we consider pursuing LEED certification. We all agreed that it would be nice to have the house recognized, and the homeowners liked the idea that the program would help us consider everything that could make the house more efficient, healthy, and sustainable. We decided to go for it, setting the LEED for Homes Gold rating as our goal. In the end, we exceeded our expectations and achieved a Platinum rating for the finished project.

Much of the criteria for LEED certification includes things that I would do on any project, but the guidelines sharpened our focus on energy-efficient construction and heathy materials. We chose to frame the house with staggered-stud walls: 2x10 plates with alternating 2x4 studs, every other stud either set to the inside or outside face of the plates to mitigate thermal bridging. We also insulated the wall cavities with mineral-wool batts—a natural alternative to fiberglass insulation.

Once we had determined to build the house on a slab, we decided to use radiant heat and planned the mechanicals around this in-floor delivery system. There are three components to the house's simple mechanical system: an air-to-water heat pump, an on-demand electric water heater, and a heat-recovery ventilator (HRV). The heat pump also preheats the water heater supply. The HRV completely exchanges the home's air every four hours, preheating the incoming air to reduce energy loss. These and other energy-efficiency measures landed us in the "Exceptional Energy Performance" category as we calculated LEED points.

We used daylighting strategies to reduce the electric loads while the sun is up and LED light fixtures throughout the house for the times of day when sunlight isn't available. The house is outfitted with water-efficient plumbing fixtures, though gaining points in this category meant verifying that Canadian fixtures, rated in liters per minute, met LEED's gallon-per-minute requirements.

Not only did the building site offer LEED points for being an existing infill lot near public transport, but we gained points for not being in a flood plain, wetland, or environmentally sensitive area, and for being close to community resources. We earned points for a landscape plan that includes food production, drought-tolerant plantings, and permeable surfaces. We also gained points based on third-party verification of the home's durability and ventilation strategies. Other efforts to keep indoor air quality healthy—some as simple as designing a place to leave shoes at the door—also led to our Platinum rating.

But the real secret to sustainability is realizing that great things come in small packages. At 1,200 sq. ft., there is simply less home to consume resources and energy.

THE TALK OF THE TOWN

I have a friend who has been working and living in and around Squamish since the '50s. He says, "If you want to do something different, do something well." That was our mantra for this project. In fact, the most unique aspect of this house is how simple and traditional it looks from the outside.

Located less than a few miles away is a subdivision filled with dozens of sleek, new modern homes, yet somehow our simple and honest home has been the talk of the town and has been visited by hundreds of people during a few home tours we've been honored to be involved in.

It's always worth reflecting on completed work, but when looking back on this project, it's hard to say what we might have done differently. If I were to change anything during the process, it would be to spend more time encouraging the local planners to really rethink the suburban design standards and encourage more small homes. But I'll let the house itself speak to that issue.

PURPOSEFULLY PLANNED PROPERTY

At 33 ft. by 120 ft., not only is the property
small, but the back of the lot also has an existing
building that the homeowners wanted to keep. This
pushed the house to the front setback, leaving
just enough space for raised vegetable beds and
parking in the front yard and a small patio and
gardens in the back. Drainage is directed into a
dry riverbed that traverses the backyard, which is
packed with shade-tolerant native plantings. Where
the site has sun, the architect chose water-smart
perennials and ornamental grasses. The native and
drought-tolerant plants, permeable surfaces, and
dedicated places for food production earned points
towards the LEED Platinum certification.

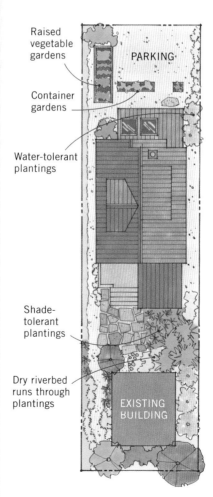

Raised
vegetable
gardens

PARKING

Container
gardens

Water-tolerant
plantings

Shade-
tolerant
plantings

Dry riverbed
runs through
plantings

EXISTING
BUILDING

TEXAS HOMESTEAD REVIVED

A sagging 1800s farm-house is shored up with salvaged materials to enhance its rustic character

BY KYLIE JACQUES

BUILT IN 1904, THIS IS ONE OF THE ORIGINAL FARM-houses found along Old Austin Highway. Its uninsulated plank construction—top plate, bottom plate, and 1x12s with battens—was less familiar to designer/builder Richard Laughlin than the framing he typically sees. "The house is just 30 miles away from most of our jobs, but it was built in a totally different era," he says. "People were poor and they had to make do with what they had." To strengthen the walls, Laughlin added infill framing, creating an insulation cavity as well as a wiring cavity. The floor system was in bad shape, too. It sat on a stacked-rock foundation—the joists were either in the rubble or sitting on soil and, like the sills and subfloor, were in various stages of rot. To stabilize the structure and seal for moisture control, Laughlin pulled up the entire floor, leveled the building, and excavated to pour a concrete slab with foundation footings to support point loads inside the building. He replaced the joists with 2x4 sleepers over the new slab and reinstalled the original hardwood floorboards to be in keeping with the period.

"When we are working on these old houses, we try to go back in with period-appropriate materials to match the patina of the original products."
—Richard Laughlin, designer/builder

Designer/builder: Laughlin Homes +
Restoration,
hillcountrybuilder.com
Location: Johnson City, Texas
Photos: Sarah Moore-Natsumi,
courtesy of Laughlin Homes +
Restoration

Part 3

OTHER SMALL STRUCTURES

SMART STORAGE FOR SMALL SPACES

Add convenience and comfort to small kitchens and baths

BY PATRICK MCCOMBE

LIVING IN A SMALL HOUSE REQUIRES MAKING THE most of any potential storage space, particularly in the kitchen or bathroom. With the right kind of storage, you can prevent the clutter that makes these spaces feel cramped and unkempt, as well as the frustration that goes with it. Instead, you'll have spaces that are tidy and that feel larger than their square footage would indicate. What follows is a collection of the very best storage solutions we've come across in the last few years. As you go through the next few pages, you'll find that even the very smallest spaces can be put to good use, and you'll see that smart storage is often more about better organization than it is about creating additional space. We hope you'll use these ideas as inspiration for your own projects. If you come up with your own creative storage solution, please send us a photo. If we like what we see, we might include it in a future issue.

BREAKFAST BOOTH, CHINA CABINET

Despite its modest proportions, this kitchen feels larger than it is. One reason is the built-in booth beneath a bank of windows. The seat back is affixed to full-extension drawer slides, allowing it to glide upward to reveal generous storage spaces. Cabled counterweights make it easy to lift the sliding panel. A drawer in the top of the booth claims the rest of the space.

Architects: Arkin Tilt Architects, Berkeley, Calif.; arkintilt.com
Cabinetmakers: Bryan Harris and Greg Tolman, Emeryville, Calif.

DINING-ROOM DESK

A chest-high buffet cabinet separates the dining area from the kitchen in this house. The buffet turned out to be the perfect place to tuck an old-fashioned flip-down desktop in the service of 21st-century technology.

Designer/builder: Chris Stebbins, Eugene, Ore.
Cabinets: The Cabinet Factory, Eugene, Ore.; thecabinetfactoryeugene.com

KITCHEN LAPTOP DRAWER

The kids eat their breakfast at this windowsill-height counter next to the kitchen cabinets. Once they are off to school, Mom pulls the laptop out of the drawer built into the side of the base cabinet, grabs a cup of coffee, and gets to work. An electric outlet in the base cabinet provides the power.

Designer/builder: Paul Johnson, Portland, Ore.; pauljohnsoncarpentry.com

CLEVER CABINET

This efficient, highly functional cabinet is a key part of a redesigned farmhouse kitchen. The front of the unit houses the home phone. Above the phone are mail slots and open shelving. Below is a pullout drawer with an outlet for charging cell phones. The cabinet side contains a whiteboard with marker storage, a corkboard, key hooks, and angled slots for school papers.

Designer: Dana Frey, Starline Cabinets, Chilliwack, B.C.; starlinecabinets.com

TUCK AWAY THE TOASTER

Storage space was limited in this compact modern kitchen, so San Francisco–based Hulburd Design invented a slide-out plywood platform behind the microwave to support a toaster and a coffeemaker. The two appliances are behind a bright-red door that opens with a touch latch. Hiding these appliances reduces clutter and increases prep space on the butcher-block countertop.

Designer: Hulburd Design, San Francisco, hulburddesign.com

NARROW VANITY FOR TWO

The cabinet that contains this farm-house sink is narrower than a traditional double vanity, so it takes up less room in a small bath. Even with a space-saving vanity, the sink's ample size keeps water contained and provides enough room for sharing. The vanity's glass pulls and the sink's two cross-handle faucets maintain a look that's consistent with the home's Tudor style and vintage.

Designer: Ann McCulloch, Portland, Ore.

HIDEAWAY KITCHEN TABLE

When his Montauk, N.Y., clients requested a pullout table to seat extra dinner guests, Chris Greenawalt came up with a two-legged steel table that slides in and out of a chase between the countertop and the cabinets below. A steel plate bolted to the end of the table prevents it from coming out altogether.

Designer: Chris Greenawalt, Charlestown, Mass.; bunkerworkshop.com

A SIMPLE SCREENED PORCH

Inexpensive screen panels combined with cable railings create a clever assembly

BY ANDY ENGEL

BRIAN KELLEY'S COMPANY, FUSION RENOVATIONS, Inc., was building a new home on a ridge overlooking upstate New York's rural Harlem Valley when his clients decided to add insect screening to the porch. This isn't an uncommon request, and over the years I've seen carpenters tackle this project in many ways. The most common solutions seem to be either filling the spa–olling screening across the assembly and securing it with trim strips. But wood can rot, and there's no elegant way to repair future damage to screen that does not have an individual frame.

Brian and carpenter Eric Paulson took a simple approach to avoid these issues. They used the existing posts to anchor aluminum-framed screens purchased from Metro Screenworks (metroscreenworks.com). In this case, the homeowners knew they would be leaving the screens in place year-round, so fastening them from the outside made sense. But for a more convertible approach, the screen panels could be secured to the inside of the cedar stops. Because cable railings had been installed every-where else on the existing deck to preserve the incredible view to the west, it was an easy decision to continue these railings around the porch as well. Screens are only intended to keep out bugs, but a screened porch built to code will also keep people from falling.

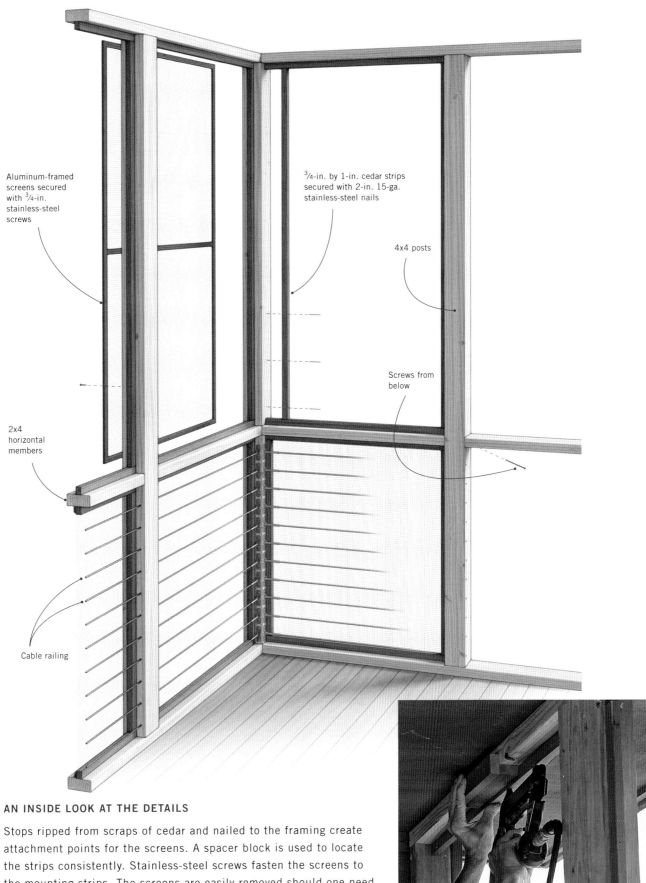

Aluminum-framed
screens secured
with ¾-in.
stainless-steel
screws

¾-in. by 1-in. cedar strips
secured with 2-in. 15-ga.
stainless-steel nails

4x4 posts

Screws from
below

2x4
horizontal
members

Cable railing

AN INSIDE LOOK AT THE DETAILS

Stops ripped from scraps of cedar and nailed to the framing create attachment points for the screens. A spacer block is used to locate the strips consistently. Stainless-steel screws fasten the screens to the mounting strips. The screens are easily removed should one need repairs. If seasonal removal of the screens had been desired, the screens could have been mounted from inside for easier removal.

BUILD A BUDGET-FRIENDLY SHED

Get ample storage and traditional styling on a budget

BY JUSTIN FINK

CALL ME A BUILDING SNOB IF YOU WANT, BUT I think most sheds are ugly. The response when I say this to people is usually, "Yeah, but who cares what it looks like if it gets the job done?"

In some ways, I agree. I have no problem with an ultracheap or even downright homely storage shed that is being built just to keep tools and equipment out of the weather. But why settle for an oddly proportioned, poorly built shed that isn't durable, is adorned with appliques that don't match the main house (or even the region of the country the shed is located in), and doesn't offer enough storage space or the right type of access to suit its purpose—especially when even the smallest of these lackluster factory-built sheds cost thousands of dollars?

I challenged myself to design a shed that provides lots of storage but that can be built for a low price. To meet the needs of most homeowners, a shed must be bigger than 8x10 or even 10x12, so I set my sights on a 10x16 structure. For the budget, I set a goal of $2,000*, which I knew would be difficult to meet. The final challenge: The shed had to look better than the low-pitched, cheaply clad, cookie-cutter models being sold at most big-box stores and shed retailers.

"Look better" is, of course, subjective. My personal taste leans toward a traditional style, so I took cues from tobacco barns and other New England farm-style outbuildings in my area while relying on as few obviously modern building materials as possible. It may sound crazy, but I wanted to enjoy the interior of my shed as much as the exterior, and as long as it would keep out rain and snow, I didn't mind it being leaky enough to let in streaks of sunlight. To that end, I decided to forgo the convenience and strength of sheet goods and used rough-sawn, knotty, 1x8 spruce boards for many parts of this shed, leaving them unfinished so that they eventually would weather to a pleasant gray. If you want to streamline the process and aren't concerned about achieving a true old-fashioned look, then by all means go for OSB or plywood. It probably will save you money compared to the solid-wood alternatives I sourced, not to mention that it will simplify the wall bracing. Some panel goods, such as T1-11, even double as finished siding.

Speaking of simplicity, it's good to set reasonable expectations for a project like this. Every project boils down to a balance between time, money, and quality. This build will save you some money, but you won't be able to crank it out in a couple of days. I wasn't trying to turn a profit here, so when I could shave off a few bucks by putting in some extra

*Prices may have changed since original publication in 2016.

legwork and using slightly warped or otherwise wonky materials (such as the 1x8s), I was perfectly willing. Likewise, if I could have fun making my own barn-door hardware to save $50, that was a win-win. In fact, aside from the windows that I picked up years ago from the side of the road (you can buy affordable equivalents from betterbarns.com), I built this entire project using materials from my local big-box store.

PROPER PROPORTIONS

A bit of planning and some measured drawings are crucial to ensuring that you don't end up with an oddly proportioned backyard eyesore. I like to design using SketchUp (a free design program available online), which makes it easy to draw a basic shape and to adjust the height and width of walls, the height and pitch of the roof, the depth of overhangs, and the size and placement of doors and windows. Whether you use a design program or just some graph paper, you can experiment with changes to work out problems before you put on your toolbelt.

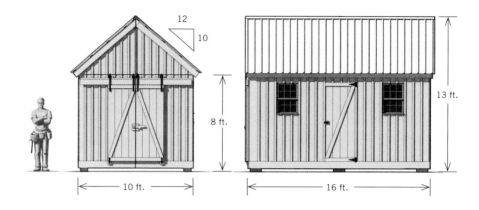

A DURABLE ROOF

Metal panels last long and look traditional, and although they required a special order from my local big-box store, they were nearly the same price as architectural shingles. They made it possible for me to use skip sheathing on the roof rather than continuous sheathing. As an added benefit, I was able to install the corrugated panels faster than I would have been able to lay shingles.

LOTS OF ACCESS

A big door on the gable end accommodates a lawn tractor and other wheeled items. A smaller door on the eave wall offers access when I need hand tools and other items. This setup alleviates the common problem of having to move multiple items to reach the one you want.

WOOD WINDOWS

Single-pane, true divided-lite wood windows not only look better than vinyl products, but they are about the same price. If you can't find such windows at a local yard sale, recycling station, salvage yard, or building-supply store, or if repurposing isn't your thing, try betterbarns.com for affordable options. Here, I repurposed some old sashes.

TRADITIONAL BOARD-AND-BATTEN SIDING

Here, I used full 1x8 spruce for the boards, and rip cuts from the same stock as battens to pin the board edges and allow for expansion. To keep the bottom ends of the battens from wicking ground moisture and rotting prematurely, I had them land on a skirtboard rather than running all the way to the bottom edge of the building.

A HYBRID FRAME FOR A CLASSIC LOOK

In many ways, this shed is built like a standard house, with dimensional-lumber framing for the floor, walls, and roof. But because the design uses boards where panel sheathing normally would be, it was necessary to incorporate some traditional bracing to strengthen the frame and to provide solid nailing for the siding and the roof panels.

1 BRACING STRATEGY

Ideally, the diagonal bracing would be continuous on both eave walls of the shed, but even though it's interrupted by window openings, it still does its job. If your interior storage plans don't include using the space between studs, consider notching the bracing into the studs for an even stronger frame and faster girt installation.

2 BUDGET BOARDS

The heroes of this build are the inexpensive rough-sawn spruce 1x8s used for floor sheathing, siding boards, and door panels, and ripped into narrower strips for girts, battens, bracing, and trim.

3 A 2-FT. GRID

Walls are laid out on a rough 2-ft. grid, with studs and horizontal girts spaced 24 in. on center to provide nailing for the siding. Most of the girts are ripped from the 1x8 rough-sawn spruce, but the upper parts of each gable have 2x girts so that the upper siding can lap easily over the lower siding.

HOMEMADE DOOR HARDWARE

I made the roller hardware for this shed's barn doors myself, using a variety of locally purchased components. The savings were marginal compared to prefab farm-grade track hardware, but much greater compared to barn-door hardware with the type of traditional look I wanted.

For the wheels, I chose 3-in. swivel pulleys and cut off the swivel portion of the pulley assembly. I bent and hammered a piece of ¼-in. bar stock into an L-shape, then drilled and painted it. Finally, I attached the wheel and housing to the bar with a bolt and a long clevis pin. The wheel and strap assemblies ride along the edge of the track, which is just a piece of ¼-in. by 1½-in. steel angle. To keep the bottom of the door from swinging outward, I used a type of fence catch meant to accommodate a 2x4 door bar, furring it off the building so that it would fit the thicker door (not shown).

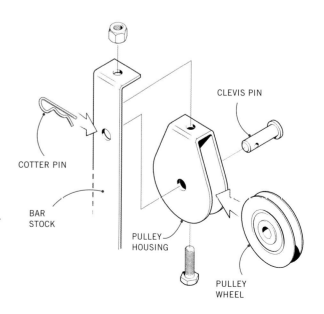

COTTER PIN

CLEVIS PIN

BAR STOCK

PULLEY HOUSING

PULLEY WHEEL

BUILD A MODULAR MODERN WOODSHED

Designed to
be erected
in a day, this
shed uses
readily
available
materials and
basic tools

BY ROB WOTZAK

A FEW YEARS AGO, I OFFERED TO HELP A FRIEND build a woodshed in his yard. I imagined a simple rack made of 2x4s and a few sheets of metal roofing—but when I found out the shed would need to hold five cords of wood, I had to adjust my plans. The design I came up with is easy to scale up or down, as I did for the much smaller shed shown in this article.

Ideally, a woodshed is sized just tall enough to comfortably walk inside to stack firewood. With a shed roof, the deeper the structure, the taller it needs to be. A cord of stacked firewood takes up 128 cu. ft.—basically a 4-ft. by 4-ft. by 8-ft. pile. When planning your own shed, choose a height and floor layout that works for you, but don't forget to consider adding a decent roof overhang on the front for extra protection from the elements.

This shed measures 5 ft. deep, 8 ft. wide, and 8 ft. tall, so I was able to use standard-size framing lumber with minimal waste, but you can build whatever size fits the number of cords you want to store and the space you have in your yard. The basic steps are outlined below and shown in detail in the photos that follow.

PREP THE SITE AND THEN CUT THE PARTS

There are a few different ways to prepare the shed base. For the shed featured here, which is small in size, I opted for a grid of concrete blocks set in gravel. Another option is to lay a bed of tamped gravel, which provides a dry, mud-free site to build on. (Plus, you don't have to get fussy when raising and leveling the shed—if one sill beam is a little low, just lift it and rake some gravel under it.)

LAY THE FLOOR

I've found that if I choose appropriate spacing for the floor beams, then 2x4s are plenty strong for a shed floor. Because this shed sits right on the ground with nothing to hold each of its beams in position, the floor boards keep the base square.

ERECT THE WALLS

Because everything is locked in with temporary bracing, it doesn't matter which side you put up first. I'm using 5/4 PT decking for the walls because it provides a good balance of strength, thickness, and board width. Plus, it's nice-looking and straight boards are generally easy to find compared to PT 2x4s or 1x4s. I planned this shed to be exactly 8 ft. long so I could buy 8-ft. boards for the back wall without having to cut them to length.

INSTALL THE ROOF

It's easiest if you design your shed to use standard-length metal roofing panels. My local lumberyard carries galvanized metal in 8-ft. and 12-ft. panels, which are ideal, but for this project I needed to cut sheets on site.

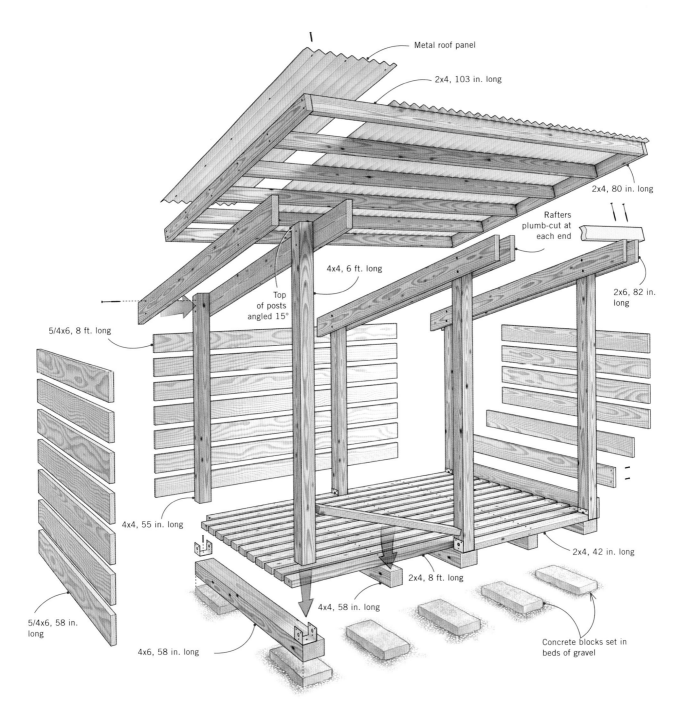

Metal roof panel

2x4, 103 in. long

2x4, 80 in. long

Rafters plumb-cut at each end

2x6, 82 in. long

4x4, 6 ft. long

Top of posts angled 15°

5/4x6, 8 ft. long

4x4, 55 in. long

5/4x6, 58 in. long

4x6, 58 in. long

4x4, 58 in. long

2x4, 8 ft. long

2x4, 42 in. long

Concrete blocks set in beds of gravel

SKETCH IT OUT

The design of this structure is fairly simple, so if you're an experienced carpenter, you might be able to do a little math to figure out the important dimensions, jot down some numbers, and just start building. I decided to use the free 3D modeling software from SketchUp to draw a full plan so I could quickly figure out a layout I liked for the walls and which roof angle looked right, but drawing a simple plan with a ruler, pencil, and paper would have worked as well.

MODULAR METHOD

The design can be scaled up or down. Making additional bents is simplified by the assembly-style approach.

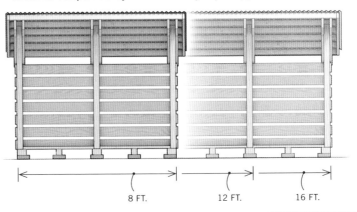

8 FT.   12 FT.   16 FT.

MATERIALS LIST

FOUNDATION
(8) 50-lb. bags of gravel
(10) 4x8x16 solid-concrete blocks

FLOOR
(1) 4x6x16, PT
(1) 4x4x10, PT
(13) 2x4x8, PT
(6) 4x4 galvanized post bases
(1) Box Simpson Strong-Tie #9 1½-in.
Structural-Connector Screws (100-count)
(1) 5-lb. box 3-in. galvanized deck screws

POSTS/RAFTERS
(3) 4x4x12, PT
(6) 2x6x8, PT
(1) Box FastenMaster Headlok 4½-in. Heavy-Duty
Flathead Fasteners (50-count)

WALLS
(7) 5/4x6x8 PT deck board
(7) 5/4x6x10 PT deck board
(1) 5-lb. box 2½-in. galvanized
deck screws

ROOF
(6) 2x4x10, PT
(2) 2x4x8, PT
(5) Union Corrugating 2.16-ft. by
8-ft. Corrugated Metal Roof
Panels
(1) Box Teks #9 Self-Drilling
Roofing Screws (400-count)

PREP THE SITE

DIG FOOTINGS. Set and level solid concrete blocks on compacted gravel to support the ends of each of the floor beams.

CUT THE PARTS

CUT FLOOR BEAMS TO LENGTH. The shed depth and resulting beam length are based on how many courses of firewood you want to fit in the shed—in this case, three. Consider the proportions that will look good and use a common board length that will leave little waste after being cut to size. Make two passes with a circular saw for the cuts.

FIGURE OUT POST LENGTHS. Mark and cut the tops of the front and rear posts to match the height and pitch of the roof. If you did an accurate drawing, you should be able to pull the lengths and cut angles right from it, but you can also lay the posts out on the ground with a sill beam, a rafter, and a tape measure and mark your cuts in place.

LEFT: CUT POSTS. Flush-mounted rafters are held in place with TimberLok screws because the rafters are just supporting a lightweight metal roof. If this method won't pass code where you live, mark and cut 1½-in. notches at the tops of the posts.

BELOW: ATTACH POST BASES. Fasten the bases to the ends of the beams. Put them all the way to the edge for the side beams and center the hardware on the center beam. To keep things simple, these post bases are installed with screws rather than bolts.

ASSEMBLE THE BENTS

IN HINDSIGHT... You will attach the posts while the sill beams are lying on their sides, so learn from my mistake and orient the hardware so the fastening flanges are on the front and back instead of the sides—otherwise you will have to flip the whole assembly over to drive the screws on one side of the base.

CUT AND SECURE RAFTERS. Once the posts are squarely attached to the beams, cut the rafters to length and fasten them at the top of the posts, leaving the desired overhang on each end.

RAISE AND REPEAT

LIFT THE FIRST SECTION. The first completed bent should sit on the first pair of concrete blocks with the posts flush with the outside edges.

PLUMB THE POSTS. Attach temporary diagonal bracing to keep the shed frame plumb and square until there are enough floor and wall boards attached to lock everything in place. Keep the bracing completely inside the perimeter of the shed on the back posts so it won't be in the way when installing the walls.

LAY THE FLOOR

LAY INTERMEDIATE FLOOR BEAMS. There is no beam on the front or back of the shed and no true floor joists. With this system, you raise the main frame sections, drop the additional beams in between, and screw down the 2x floor boards to tie everything together.

FASTEN FLOOR BOARDS. Attach the 2x4s at the front and back, putting two 3-in. screws into the boards where they cross each beam. Infill with enough floor boards to leave 1-in. gaps for airflow to help dry the firewood. Use 1-in.-thick scraps to space them out as you fasten them down.

ERECT THE WALLS

PUT ON THE SIDES. The wall boards go up in the same fashion as the floor boards. Put a 2x4 scrap at each end to create a 1½-in. gap and lay the next course, then fasten the boards with 2½-in. screws at each post. Using spacer blocks means there's no need to measure when laying out the courses. Plan the height so the top of the wall will finish with a full-width board.

RIGHT: FASTEN PURLINS.
Set each 2x4 purlin on
edge and then fasten them
into the tops of the rafters
with HeadLok structural
screws. Because the shed's
metal roofing runs from
front to back, the rafters
act more like beams to
support the horizontal
purlins.

FAR RIGHT: TRIM DETAIL.
Fasten a 2x4 board to the
ends of the purlins to finish
off both sides of the roof
framing.

INSTALL THE ROOF

CUTTING SHEETS ON SITE. Clamp a board or
other straight edge onto the entire stack of panels
and use a metal-cutting blade in a circular saw to
make quick and clean cuts in the roof panels.

SCREW SHEETS TO FRAMING. Use self-tapping
metal-roofing screws to fasten the panels to the
purlins. These screws have silicone or rubber gas-
kets to prevent leaks. Refer to the manufacturer's
fastening schedule for the ideal spacing.

ADD REMAINING PANELS. Work from one end of the
roof to the other, following the roofing manufacturer's
guidelines for panel overlap and fastener layout.

BUILD A GATEWAY PERGOLA

This cedar structure combines the look of traditional joinery with contemporary lines—all built with simple techniques

BY JUSTIN FINK

WHEN MY FRIEND BRIAN STARTED TALKING ABOUT building an outdoor structure to create a threshold between his short gravel parking area and the front yard of his house, it was clear that a large pergola would be the ideal solution. Set atop a timber retaining wall and flanked by plantings, the pergola would create an informal, open gateway.

But, like any other widely available, mass-produced outdoor structure, store-bought pergolas have begun to suffer from inelegant designs, sub-par materials, and haphazard assembly methods that place a high value on convenience at the expense of durability. I knew we could do better, so we set out to design a custom alternative. The design we came up with reflects Brian's contemporary, Asian-inspired taste, and could be built by anybody, regardless of whether they have access to the large timbers or specialized tools needed to erect a true timber-frame structure.

START WITH A STYLE IN MIND

The pergola would become the first thing seen and passed through on the way to the house, so it needed to mesh with the architectural style of the home, which had been remodeled to have a somewhat contemporary exterior—lap siding mixed with vertical siding, paint mixed with natural wood, and several levels of landscaping, hardscaping, and attached structures. The look leans towards an Asian aesthetic, which also happens to be the basis of the Arts and Crafts style. So, it made sense to build on this concept by including the look of traditional mortise and tenon joinery and clean, square edges. The contemporary feel came into play with the incorporation of some Asian design elements—subtle curves, recessed purlins, and crisp horizontal lines—which became a good opportunity to deal with crucial issues of proportion. Because the space demanded a fairly large structure, we worked hard to keep it looking well rooted with a sleek, airy feel for the upper portion, flowing down to a substantial base.

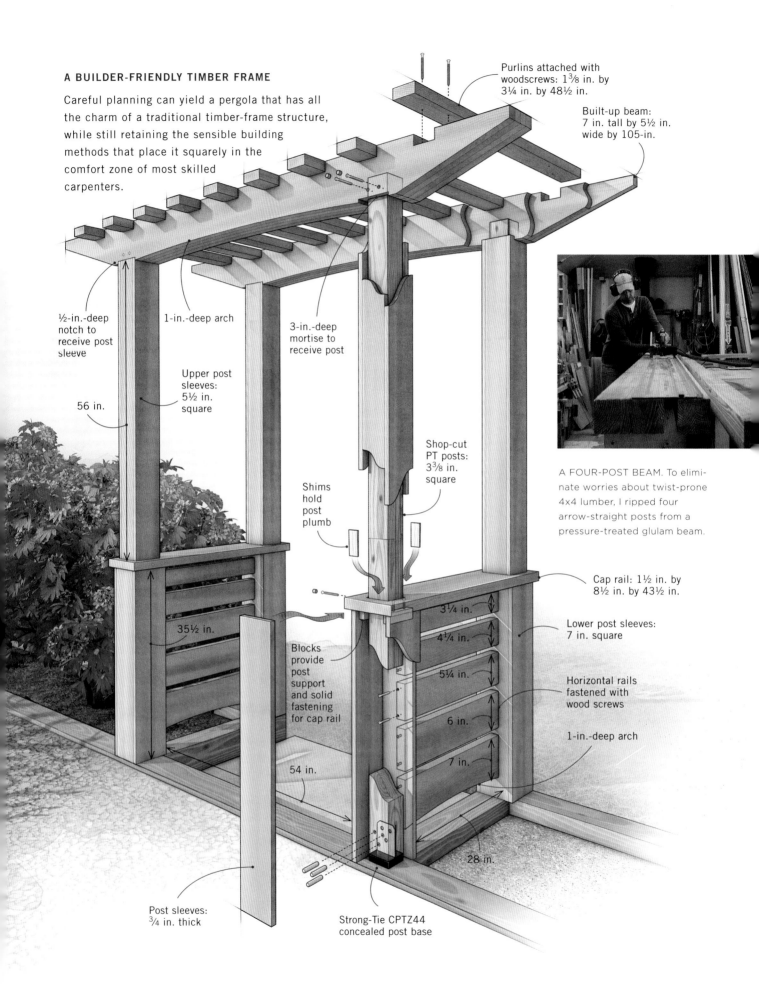

A BUILDER-FRIENDLY TIMBER FRAME

Careful planning can yield a pergola that has all the charm of a traditional timber-frame structure, while still retaining the sensible building methods that place it squarely in the comfort zone of most skilled carpenters.

Purlins attached with woodscrews: 1⅜ in. by 3¼ in. by 48½ in.

Built-up beam: 7 in. tall by 5½ in. wide by 105-in.

½-in.-deep notch to receive post sleeve

1-in.-deep arch

3-in.-deep mortise to receive post

Upper post sleeves: 5½ in. square

56 in.

Shop-cut PT posts: 3⅜ in. square

Shims hold post plumb

A FOUR-POST BEAM. To eliminate worries about twist-prone 4x4 lumber, I ripped four arrow-straight posts from a pressure-treated glulam beam.

Cap rail: 1½ in. by 8½ in. by 43½ in.

35½ in.

Blocks provide post support and solid fastening for cap rail

3¼ in.

4¼ in.

5¼ in.

6 in.

7 in.

Lower post sleeves: 7 in. square

Horizontal rails fastened with wood screws

1-in.-deep arch

54 in.

28 in.

Post sleeves: ¾ in. thick

Strong-Tie CPTZ44 concealed post base

BUILT-UP BEAMS. Unlike solid 6x8 cedar, shop-laminated cedar beams allow the individual plies to be cut and curved without a large bandsaw or timber-framing tools. The curve comes first. After aligning the ¼-in. plywood router template to the top edge and centerpoint of the 2x beam ply, mark the curve and cut wide of the line with a jigsaw.

TAPERS WITH A TRACKSAW. With the curve marked, lay out the rest of the beam with a framing square before cutting the tapers on either end of each ply with a track-guided circular saw.

BLUNT THE BEAM ENDS. After cutting all the tapers, remove the point of each beam ply. These cuts don't have to be exact, as they'll get cleaned up after the plies have been laminated.

ABOVE LEFT AND RIGHT: BEARING-GUIDED CLEANUP. After rough-cutting each 2x, realign and attach the template with double-stick carpet tape, then set the depth of a spiral-cutting, bearing-guided router bit to ride on the edge of the ¼-in. plywood.

RIP THE REMAINDER. Set the tablesaw fence to a 7-in. rip cut to trim the excess from the bottom of each beam ply, creating flat spots where the posts will later meet each assembled beam.

DON'T BE SHY WITH THE GLUE. Spread a thick coat of exterior wood glue—as much for sealing the wood between pieces as it is for adhering them—across both mating surfaces before joining the pieces and securing them with screws every 4 in. around the perimeter.

CLAMPS ASSEMBLE PAIRS. After the glue holding each pair of plies has set, back out the screws used to clamp the pieces, then glue and clamp pairs together with screw holes facing inward where they will not be seen.

SAND AND SHAPE. Don't fuss over perfect alignment during glue-up. Use 10 minutes and some 80-grit sandpaper for the inevitable task of blending and smoothing seams.

MATERIALS AND METHODS THAT MAKE SENSE

A conventional solution for building a post-and-beam-style pergola like this one would be to use—you guessed it—solid wood posts and beams. But solid timbers require traditional joinery, and that means lots of time spent on mortises. This wouldn't be a dealbreaker on a simple four-post, two-beam pergola, but our design included five horizontal rails that would need to be mortised between pairs of posts, upper posts of different dimensions than the lower posts, and a wide cap rail on each side that would have to tie into the posts with through-mortises.

Although it didn't offer much cost savings (cedar is expensive no matter how you slice it), I set aside the idea of solid posts and beams and instead opted to laminate more commonly available 2x cedar to create the top beams, which I

TIMBER-FRAME-STYLE JOINERY. With the help of some common power tools, you can add the feel of timber-frame joinery to the beams without too much traditional fuss. Start with the notches for the post sleeves. Use a simple router template to guide a router collet and mortising bit, creating notches where the upper post sleeves will attach to the beams.

FORSTNER FOLLOWED BY A CHISEL. The fastest low-tech method for making deep mortises is to drill holes with a Forstner-style drill bit, then remove the waste with a chisel and mallet.

A DADO FOR EACH PURLIN. After taping each side of the beam to prevent tearout, make a series of parallel, circular saw cuts to rough out a dado for each purlin, which are then quick and easy to knock free with a hammer or bend and break with a chisel or pry bar.

BEARING-GUIDED CLEANUP. With the bulk of the waste out of the way, smooth the bottom of each dado with a bearing-guided bit, which rides along the shoulders of the cutout to get tight into the corners.

then set atop pressure-treated posts wrapped in 1x cedar. This approach allowed me to install the rails faster, eliminated worries about tying the cap rails into the posts, simplified the required tools and the process of shaping the curved beams, and gave me complete control over the apparent width of the posts, which could now run uninterrupted from base to beam.

Choosing a material for the structural posts was a challenge, though. Any builder who has worked with pressure-treated 4x4s knows they are prone to twisting, and that movement would wreak havoc on this assembly. In an effort to find a stable, rot-resistant, affordable solution, I ordered a pressure-treated glulam beam from my lumberyard, which I then ripped into four arrow-straight posts that would be far less likely to twist.

HOLLOW ASSEMBLY CREATES A SUBSTANTIAL BASE. To beef up the appearance of the structural 4x4 shop-cut posts, I used wide, hollow post sleeves infilled with wide horizontal rails and a substantial cap rail. Start the lower half of each side of the pergola by assembling the butt-jointed post sleeves, which are left open on one side to allow access to attach the rails and, later, to secure the hidden 4x4 posts to their bases.

KEEP THE RAILS SIMPLE. Drive a pair of screws through the post sleeves into the endgrain of each horizontal rail to hold them tight, in line, and on layout, ensuring their position with a spacer board under the rails and a ¼-in. spacer block between each end.

MAKE WAY FOR THE POSTS. Drill a ½-in. hole on either side of the cap rail to provide access for a jigsaw to make each square post-hole cutout without resorting to an awkward plunge cut.

FASTEN THE CAP. After adding blocks to hold the posts steady in the oversized sleeves and to provide fastening for the cap-rail screws, add a spacer to ensure the open sides of the sleeves are held to the right width before fastening from above where the screws will be hidden by the upper post sleeves.

PREFAB PARTS ASSEMBLE EASILY ON SITE. If the shop portion goes as planned, you can arrive on site with two nearly complete lower assemblies, four posts and upper sleeves, two beams, a stack of purlins, and a fairly straightforward half-day of work. To start, clamp the CPTZ44 post-base bracket to the post, using it as a template for boring the holes to receive the metal pins.

EASY KERFS. Make parallel passes with a circular saw on both sides of the post to create the $3/16$-in. kerf necessary to receive the vertical fin of the base bracket.

SET THE BASES. Pan-head structural screws provide a quick connection between the post base and the timber retaining wall.

PINS FOR THE WIN. Unlike conventional post bases, these allow the posts to be fastened from one side, so the lower assembly can already be in place.

The posts would be secured to the timber retaining wall via 4x4 post bases, but in order to ease this process I chose Simpson Strong-Tie CPTZ44 concealed post bases that use metal through-pins installed from one side rather than the traditional post bases that require nails or screws driven from two sides. This meant I could assemble most of the wrapped posts in the shop—leaving just one side off each post—and I would still have all the access I'd need for securing the posts to the post bases.

PREFABRICATION AND PREP WORK

The tools required for building this pergola aren't exotic, so there's no reason the whole job can't be done right on site if desired. Personally, anytime I have the option to build a project in the shop versus doing the work on site, I choose the shop. Having my tools organized and close at hand means a faster, more efficient workflow. In this case it was an added convenience, as I prefabricated as much of the pergola as I could on cold late-winter days in

SHIM IT PLUMB. Using a long level, plumb each post in both directions and hold them in place with shims. Cut the shims flush to prevent interference with the upper post sleeves.

TOP AND ABOVE: SEALED CONNECTION. After masking off the surrounding cap rail, apply a bead of marine adhesive sealant, then slide the upper post sleeve into place and tack it with finish nails.

anticipation of an only slightly warmer early-spring installation.

The goal was to leave the shop with subassemblies of parts that could then be put together in place. I started with the top beams, which were the most labor-intensive part of the build. I laminated each of the two beams from four 2x8s that I individually rough-cut and then curved with a template-guided router before joining them together with a healthy coating of waterproof exterior wood glue. Once the beams were glued up, I did the fit and finish work, including thoroughly sanding with both 80-grit and 100-grit sandpaper and creating pockets for post sleeves and mortises

for the posts themselves as well as dadoes across the top of the beams to receive the purlins.

Everything below the beams and purlins can be broken down into a pair of lower halves and a pair of upper halves. The lower halves consist of wide post sleeves and horizontal rails, which are crowned with a hefty cap rail with jigsaw-cut square holes. These square holes allow the shop-cut 4x4 posts to slide into the lower assemblies and be attached to the post bases once on site. Then the upper post sleeves can be slid onto the posts before the beams are installed.

The on-site assembly work started with locating and setting the concealed post bases, being sure to orient each so that when the lower assem-

LEFT: FINISH THE BASE. Coat the edges of each remaining post sleeve, slide them into place, and fasten with finish nails.

MIDDLE AND ABOVE: BEAMS DROP ON. Apply sealant to the top of each post sleeve, then lower the beams into place and fasten them to the posts, bunging the holes for a clean, finished look.

PURLINS COME LAST. Tap each purlin into place and fasten with exterior wood screws, which are then covered with a smear of adhesive to protect against pooling water.

blies were later dropped into place there would be access for driving the metal pins through each post before fastening the final piece of cedar on the lower sleeve. With the lower assemblies and posts located and locked into their plumb positions, it was a matter of hefting the beams up and onto the post tops, where structural screws make the per-manent connection. The last step was to drop the purlins into their dadoes.

We chose to let the cedar fade to a natural gray, but a penetrating oil would also be a suitable, rela-tively low-maintenance finish.

CONTRIBUTORS

EMORY BALDWIN, AIA, is co-owner of FabCab in Seattle, Wash.

ANNE CALLENDER is an architect in Portland, Maine

MATT COFFEY is co-owner of South Mountain Company on Martha's Vineyard in Massachusetts.

ANDY ENGEL was a senior *Fine Homebuilding* editor, a carpenter, and a freelance writer.

AARON FAGAN is a former *Fine Homebuilding* associate editor.

JUSTIN FINK is the former editorial director of *Fine Homebuilding*.

DAVID T. HARESIGN, FAIA, is a founding partner of Bonstra Haresign Architects in Washington, D.C.

MATT HUTCHINS is a principal at CAST architecture in Seattle.

PHILIP IVORY has been practicing architecture in the Philadelphia area for more than 30 years.

KILEY JACQUES is a senior editor at Green Building Advisor.

CALEB JOHNSON is the principal of Caleb Johnson Studio in Portland, Maine.

PATRICK MCCOMBE is a senior editor at *Fine Homebuilding*.

DUNCAN MCPHERSON is a principal architect with Samsel Architects in Asheville, N.C.

JON NYSTROM is an architect based in Boerne, Texas.

NIR PEARLSON, AIA, is principal architect at Nir Pearlson Architect, Inc. (green-building.com) in Eugene, Ore.

BRIAN PONTOLILO is the former editorial director of *Fine Homebuilding*.

JANICE ROHLF is a contributing editor to *Fine Homebuilding*.

MATTHEW SWETT is owner of Taproot Architects in Langley, Wash.

JAMES TUER, AIA, MAIBC, LEEDap, is an architect on Bowen Island, B.C.

ROB WOTZAK is the former editor at Fine Homebuilding.com.

ROB YAGID is the Chief Content Officer for the Taunton Press.

CREDITS

All photos are courtesy of *Fine Homebuilding* magazine © The Taunton Press, Inc. except as noted below. The articles in this book appeared in the following issues of *Fine Homebuilding*:

pp. 8–13: A Place Between by Caleb Johnson, issue 251. Photos by Trent Bell, except for photo p. 13 by Debra Judge Silber. Drawings by Martha Garstang Hill.

pp. 14–21: A New Build with Sentimental Charm by Kiley Jacques, issue 309. Photos by Susan Teare. Site-plan drawing courtesy of Balzer & Tuck Architecture. Floor-plan drawings by 07sketches/ Bhupeshkumar M. Malviya.

pp. 22–29: A Garden Cottage for Low-Impact Living by Nir Pearlson, issue 235. Photos © 2012 mikedeanphoto. com except for photos pp. 25-27 by Rob Yagid. Drawings by Martha Garstang Hill.

pp. 30–31: Optimizing Occupant Comfort by Kiley Jacques, issue 294. Photos by SB Studio, courtesy of New Frameworks Natural Design/Build.

pp. 32–33: Sensitive Scale, Modest Materials by Kiley Jacques, issue 292. Photos by Warren Jagger.

pp. 34–35: Durable and Efficient Island Retreat curated by Janice Rohlf, issue 304. Photos by Warren Jagger.

pp. 36–43: Stress Free in South Texas by Jon Nystrom, issue 235. Photos by Rob Yagid except for photo p. 39 by Jeff Williams. Drawings by Martha Garstang Hill.

pp. 44–51: Schoolhouse Reimagined by Rob Yagid, issue 294. Photos by Rob Yagid. Drawings by Patrick Welsh.

pp. 52–57: Carriage-House Comeback by Matt Hutchins, issue 227. Photos by Charles Miller, except for bottom right photo p. 57 by Rob Yagid. Drawings by Martha Garstang Hill.

pp. 58–59: Pivot-Point Solution by Kiley Jacques, issue 298. Photos by Rob Harrison, courtesy of Harrison Architects.

pp. 60–61: Same Square Footage, but Bigger by Kiley Jacques, issue 284. Photos by Sean Litchfield Photography.

pp. 62–69: How to Live Well With Less by Anne Callender, issue 243. Photos by Rob Yagid. Drawing by Martha Garstang Hill.

pp. 70–77: Downtown Design by James Tuer, issue 243. Photos by Rob Yagid. Drawing p. 72 by Christopher Mills; drawing p. 73 by Martha Garstang Hill; drawing p. 75 courtesy of James Tuer.

pp. 78–85: Small-Home Harmony by Matt Coffey, issue 281. Photos by Bob Gothard. Floor-plan drawing by Patrick Welsh. Construction detail drawing by John Hartman.

pp. 86–87: New Build with Traditional Character by Janice Rohlf, issue 309. Photos by Scott Bergmann Photography.

pp. 88–89: Building a Prototype by Kiley Jacques, issue 296. Photos by Michael D. Wilson.

pp. 90–95: A Mighty Hudson View by Philip Ivory, issue 259. Photos by Aaron Fagan. Drawing p. 92 by Toby Welles, WowHouse and drawings p. 93 by Martha Garstang Hill.

pp. 96–97: Fit for Floods by Kiley Jacques, issue 282. Photos by Durston Saylor.

pp. 98–105: Small House Has It All by Duncan McPherson, issue 275. Photos by Todd Crawford. Floor-plan drawings by Patrick Welsh. All other drawings by Trevor Johnston.

pp. 108–115: Sound Design by Matthew Swett, issue 275. Photos by Michael Stadler, courtesy of the homeowners. Floor-plan drawings by Patrick Welsh. Construction detail drawing by John Hartman.

pp. 116–121: Two Cabins into One by Rob Yagid, special issue 65. Photos by Anice Hoachlander, except "Before" photos courtesy of Bonstra Haresign Architects. Drawings by Martha Garstang Hill.

pp. 122–125: Magic Mountain Cabin by Aaron Fagan, special issue 51. Photos by Susan Teare. Drawings by Martha Garstang Hill.

pp. 126–133: No Dreary Days by Brian Pontolilo, issue 251. Photos by Rob Yagid. Drawing by Martha Garstang Hill.

pp. 134–141: A Fresh Take on Tradition by David T. Haresign, issue 304. Photos by Anice Hoachlander. Drawings by 07sketches/Bhupeshkumar M. Malviya.

pp. 142–143: Brand-New Old Barn curated by Janice Rohlf, issue 306. Photos by Jane Beiles Photography.

pp. 144–145: Simple Mountain Style by Janice Rohlf, issue 306. Photos by Charles Davis Smith, FAIA.

pp. 146–147: Linking the Past to the Present by Janice Rohlf, issue 302. Photos by Anice Hoachlander.

pp. 148–155: The Cabin Concept by Emory Baldwin, issue 251. Photos by Rob Yagid. Drawings by Martha Garstang Hill.

pp. 156–163: A Remarkable Home Remodel by Brian Pontolilo, issue 272. Photos by Brian Pontolilo except for "Before" and "During" photos courtesy of RisherMartin Fine Homes. Drawings by Patrick Welsh.

pp. 164–167: Magnificent Mountain Cabin by Rob Wotzak, issue 273. Photos by Susan Teare. Drawings by Bruce Morser.

pp. 168–169: Celebrating Efficient Post-and-Beam Construction curated by Kiley Jacques, issue 297. Photos by Lindsay Selin Photography.

pp. 170–175: Downsize and Simplify by Rob Yagid, issue 259. Photos by Trent Bell. Drawing courtesy of GO Logic.

pp. 176–183: A LEED House on a Small Lot by James Tuer, issue 267. Photos by Brian Pontolilo. Floor-plan drawings by Martha Garstang Hill. Construction detail drawing by Dan Thornton.

pp. 184–185: Shoring up a Flimsy Foundation and Frame curated by Kiley Jacques, issue 293. Photos by Sarah Moore-Natsumi, courtesy of Laughlin Homes + Restoration.

pp. 188–191: Smart Storage for Small Spaces compiled by Patrick McCombe, special issue 48. Photos pages 188 and 189 by Charles Miller; top photo p. 190 courtesy of Starline Cabinets; bottom photos p. 190 by Hulburd Design; top photo p. 191 courtesy of David Hiser; bottom photos p. 191 by Donovan Moran, courtesy of Chris Greenawalt.

pp. 192–193: A Simple Screened Porch by Andy Engel, issue 266. Photos by Andy Engel. Drawing by Christopher Mills.

pp. 194–197: Build a Budget-Friendly Shed by Justin Fink, issue 258. Photos by Rob Yagid. Drawings by John Hartman.

pp. 198–205: Build a Modular Modern Woodshed by Rob Wotzak, issue 288. Photos by Kiley Jacques except for photo p. 199 by Melinda Sonido. Drawings by John Hartman.

pp. 206–215: Build a Gateway Pergola by Justin Fink, issue 266. Photos by Brian Pontolilo, except photos pp. 213–215 by Rodney Diaz. Drawing by John Hartman.